How *Not* to Be
Uptight in
an Uptight World

How *Not* to Be Uptight in an Uptight World

The Message of
Jesus, James, and Peter for Today

JAMES R. TOZER

Fleming H. Revell Company
Old Tappan, New Jersey

Library of Congress Cataloging in Publication Data

Tozer, James R
    How not to be uptight in an uptight world.

    1. Christian life—Presbyterian authors. I. Title.
BV4501.2.T68   248'.48'51   75-19320
ISBN 0-8007-0759-1

TO *Vivian, my fullest joy*
TO *Lynn and David, our finest blessing*

Contents

Preface

This book is written to those who want to know more about what the Christian faith has to offer to their lives. Many people are taking a second look at themselves, where they are headed, and what they believe. Some suspect the Christian faith may have something important to say. We hope that many who are seeking will find guidance through these studies concerning some of the key insights of Jesus, James, and Peter. We will give the personal experiences of individuals who have discovered the validity of this truth for themselves.

The Christian faith is full of surprises. What it has to say to us is often neither what we expected nor what we wanted. Sometimes life gives us difficult experiences we would like to avoid. When we remain open to what God is doing we will find that His ways are not always our ways. Suddenly we will begin to sense that He is up to something and the best we can do is to seek to become alert to His initiative. An exciting sense of expectation is arising as we sense that God has quickened His pace among us at this hour.

This book is written to people who are searching and have not yet found, to those who have begun to find and want to discover more. This is written to those who are outside the Church and discouraged with its hypocrisy, emptiness, and sterility. This is written to those who have remained in the Church and are tired of the gray institutionalism where the chief chore is just to keep the machinery running.

We want to share with alive and vital Christians the exciting stories of what God is doing in dramatic ways in the lives of people and in congregations around this country. We hope to encourage, deepen, and add balance to the awakening of faith many of us find flooding the mainstream of the Church today! We hope to encourage Christ-centered commitment, social compassion, intellectual integrity, and

9

emotional growth through which the wholeness and validity of the Christian faith will be sustained among us.

A deep affection has been inspired within me for the members of Covenant Presbyterian Church, West Lafayette, Indiana. It is among these vital and gifted people that my own faith has become increasingly grounded in biblical truth. With these members of the Covenant community I have shared deep experiences of the dynamic power of God for daily living in this modern world.

I am deeply grateful to Ruth Cosler, who has typed the manuscript, and to her husband Bob, in whom we have witnessed the principles of wholeness. Gail Redfield is a loyal friend who has given countless hours to make the completion of this project possible. I am thankful for the dedicated service of Polly Tyler and Donna Starry. Lydia Sarandan is my talented colleague whose encouragement has brought rich new insights into the Christian faith. Stan Ott is my capable colleague who has built my confidence to write. For the wholeness of mind, will, and emotion I experienced in my youth I am grateful to my mother, Esther, and for a clear imperative to moral integrity I thank my father, A. G. Tozer.

At strategic moments my wife Vivian has offered the encouragement which brought the completion of this work. She has made the personal sacrifices through which time has been made available for writing. Vivian is a person in whom the wholeness of Christ's love is ever present. It has been our privilege to share deep and fulfilling experiences of God's love and power at work in our relationship. When growth in Christian faith and understanding has come it has come to us together as we have shared precious experiences and discovered new insights with Christians across America and throughout Europe. We are thankful to be sharing this Christian faith on a day-to-day basis with our children, Lynn and David. Our prayer is that they will continue to discover and enjoy the wholeness of the Christian life.

JAMES R. TOZER

Introduction

Two years ago a friend named Tom became obsessed with fear concerning himself and the large company he directs. Recently Tom was encouraging another person saying, "Problems don't have to defeat you and fill you with fear. They can become opportunities for realizing deeper strength and new achievement." As Tom faces intense difficulties today, his outlook is characterized by confidence rather than fear.

What has happened? Tom is becoming a whole person realizing the full capabilities of mind, will, and emotion rather than being torn to pieces by distressing events. First, Tom's mind was challenged with the truth of the biblical perspective concerning life's worth and destiny. Second, his life came under new management when by an act of his will he asked Christ to take charge. Finally, he became emotionally honest with himself and with God surrendering negative qualities, receiving love and strength into the depths of his being. Fear and resentment have been replaced by confidence and love.

Becoming a whole person is the continuing discovery of how to live a balanced and complete life. Such personal fulfillment is a precious quality in a time when many forces threaten to leave our lives fragmented and broken. In this book we are discussing how personal wholeness is discovered as we realize the full, dynamic potential of mind, will, and emotion.

This wholeness of mind, will, and emotion can escape us rather quickly. One Sunday afternoon I had retreated to my study to give attention to some pressing matters. The door opened slowly and there stood our ten-year-old son, David. "Hi, David!" I said.

"Daddy, is this Sunday?"

"Yes, if my memory serves me correctly, it is."

"Daddy, should you be working on Sunday?"

"Look, I'm just trying to take care of a few things."

"Daddy, it would sure be nice if you and I could do something together this afternoon."

With that I came "unglued" inside as I attempted to resolve how to meet business pressures and family needs. My mind identified the highest priority and my will supported that truth. "Sure, David, let's go!" I said.

As we went wrestling after the football, my emotions were still tied to the matters waiting on my desk. David said, "Daddy, you're not really with it, are you?" Later my feelings began to catch up with the decision of my mind and will and David had a whole person to share the afternoon with him.

"Putting it all together" is strategic to the effectiveness of a business, a football team, and a person. Balanced growth of mind, will, and emotion is essential to becoming a whole person. Groups and individuals today tend to emphasize one area of personal growth and neglect the others. Such neglect allows for a "crash" when the immature area of the personality is exposed under stress.

Our personal well-being depends upon exercising our ability to seek and know the truth. Yet, the purely intellectual person is unbalanced. Our lives are sustained by the truth only to the extent we are willing to act upon the truth we know. The extreme activist "burns out" when his compulsive efforts are based upon a limited view of the truth. Emotional dis-ease is a most distressing force today. Discovering how to deal with the emotions of fear and hostility and how to become filled with confidence and love is essential to becoming a whole person.

When we have witnessed wholeness coming into our lives and relationships we have been vividly aware that the initiator is God and that we are discovering how to be responsive to His gracious initiative toward us. The context for becoming a more complete person is Christian fellowship. Congregations are awakening to the art of building lives. Like people in the first-century Church we are being "mutually encouraged by each other's faith" (Romans 1:12). A deep sense of expectation is arising as we discover what God can do among us and as daily we witness personal victories.

The experience of becoming a whole person involves personal growth in three areas. Within the unity of the personality the Bible recognizes (1) thinking, (2) willing, and (3) feeling as activities of the whole self. Strength of character comes with balanced growth on each of these levels. This happens when what we call the mind is the whole person seeking the truth of God's Word; when what we call the will is the whole person responding to the truth of God's commandment and promise; and when what we call feeling or emotion is the whole person becoming open to the confidence and love God offers. The following is a brief summary of these three steps toward becoming a whole person to which we will be referring throughout the coming chapters.

1. *Wholeness of Mind.* The basis for personal hope is the confidence that we can know meaningful truth about ourselves and the world. One of the chief sources of inner distress today arises from our casual attitude toward truth. Many voices and many influences bombard our minds and confusion results. Jesus said, " . . . If you continue in my word, you are truly my disciples, and you will know the truth, and the truth will make you free" (John 8:31, 32). This truth will not disappoint us because God's Word offers the only adequate answers to the questions besieging our minds (*see* Romans 1:16; 5:5).

The Gospel is offensive (*see* 1 Corinthians 1:18–31) only to our presumptuous pride (*hubris*), but clearheaded reason (*ratio*) recognizes the surpassing worth of what God has spoken. God is infinite and personal; He desires to communicate with us; therefore, the Word He offers to us in Scripture is the fullest truth we can know. We become a whole person as we seek to become intellectually honest before the truth of His Word.

My friends Bob and Rachel were at the point of getting a divorce. They received advice from many people, but they came no closer to discovering the truth about themselves or the solution to their difficulties. Hope began to dawn when they humbly prayed together, "Lord, give us the desire to seek Your truth and to live in its light."

2. *Wholeness of Will.* We discover the importance of the will as we realize the difference our actions make and as we face the consequences of what we do to each other. We live in a dependable universe where moral consequences follow our decisions. Our inward turmoil arises from our inability to solve the moral dilemma of an uneasy conscience. What is required of us is written upon our hearts and our conscience bears witness (*see* Romans 2:15).

Only Christ can resolve our moral dilemma. He offers to take the full burden of our guilt, fear, and resentment upon Himself, to fill the void in our lives with His love, and to give us the strength to live according to the truth of His Word. We enter the Christian life when by an act of our will we trust what Christ can do for us and seek to become obedient to His moral imperative.

My friends Bob and Rachel began to resolve the conflict in their marriage as they began to act according to the imperatives of God's truth. They prayed together, "Lord Jesus, take charge of our lives and lead us according to Your Word." Bob continued, "Lord, I have been out of Your will and I don't want to be out of Your will any longer because it is painful."

3. *Wholeness of Emotion.* Many of us have sound ideas and good intentions but still experience deep emotional conflict. Even after Paul had entered the Christian life he cried out, "I do not understand my own actions . . . " (Romans 7:15). Here is evidence of a divided, hidden self, a force within which he could not control or understand which left him fragmented and less than whole, and which he saw Christ alone as having the power to resolve (*see* Romans 7:24). It was at this subconscious level that Paul was experiencing conflict and being drawn into actions which were difficult to understand and deeply distressing. We see Paul seeking through honest confession to bring the fragmented pieces of his inner life under the restoring power of Christ's love.

We become emotionally whole when (a) we become honest with God by confessing our secret sins and fears (*see* 1 John 1:9), (b) when we become honest with ourselves by recognizing what we are inwardly and what we can become in God's grace (*see* Proverbs 4:23), and (c) when we find Christian fellowship in which we can become honest about our deepest fears and hopes by receiving encouragement for faith and life (*see* James 5:16).

Bob and Rachel realized that there were deep, emotional hurts and hostilities they had never dared to face or resolve. In close, genuine Christian fellowship they were able to bring the deepest hurts and fears of their lives clearly and confidently before God in prayer and to receive the cleansing, restoring love of Christ into the inner depths of their lives.

The Bible sets the goal for us of coming to the fullness of stature evident in Christ (*see* Ephesians 4:13; Colossians 2:10). We are challenged by the possibility of becoming inwardly integrated and outwardly balanced as persons. In the chapters that follow we will be considering the insights Jesus, James, and Peter offer concerning how to become a whole person.

I
Principles of Wholeness
—It's Basic!—Jesus

1

The Principle of Renewal

. . . Jesus came into Galilee, preaching the gospel of God, and saying, "The time is fulfilled, and the kingdom of God is at hand; repent, and believe in the gospel."

Mark 1:14,15

All across our country we are witnessing a dynamic style of radiant, responsible, and redemptive Christianity. A renewal of faith is flooding lives and awakening congregations. Evidence of the new thing God is doing in our time is found at the grass-roots level in the Church. The conviction is arising that God intends for people to become alive and whole as persons.

People are becoming open and responsive, affirmative and supportive of each other. Evidence of the way God is quickening His pace among us is seen in the growth of small, genuinely redemptive societies in the midst of secular society. The lives of people in these fellowships are filled with meaning and they maintain decisive influence upon the entire culture.

We are learning that we cannot live, work, face life's demands, and love others without a deep, inspiring, personal faith. We are finding that Christ Himself is the One who awakens this faith and is its only sufficient center. Evidence of God's initiative in our midst is seen in the lives of young people who are swelling our congregations and are interested in Christ because of His incomparable claim and impact upon life. Laymen, pastors, and their families are tired of the cold, gray institutionalism of churches and are turning around, "turning on, " coming alive to the unlimited, unfailing source of spiritual power that is immediately available to make life complete and full.

19

In these chapters we will be discussing the biblical principles which we are discovering are the basis for becoming a whole person. Conflict plagues our society, our families, and our inner lives. We feverishly seek to ward off the political, economic, or social difficulties distressing us, but are left with the deeper apprehension that our most pressing crisis is within ourselves. Behind a mask of self-sufficiency we hide a deep anxiety. We are seriously dissatisfied with ourselves and project this inner distress upon persons and circumstances about us. Recognizing the fragmentation which has occurred within ourselves, we cherish the wholeness evident in the person of Christ. In this chapter we are considering the act of the will essential for entering the Christian life. In subsequent chapters we will discuss the intellectual and emotional growth essential to a healthy personality.

Let us focus our attention upon the person of Jesus Christ as portrayed for us in the four Gospels of the New Testament. We will be considering six principles Jesus gives as the basis for the wholeness of the Christian life. These principles are His action plan for bringing life, hope, and joy to our lives and to society. We have Mark's portrait of Jesus beginning His life's work. He is taking the first step toward realizing His final objective. He is now initiating whatever He will accomplish on this earth. What is the first thing He does? He sets forth the principle of renewal.

If our tired, anxious, despairing lives are going to have strength, vitality, and meaning we must be renewed deeply from within by some regenerating force. Some people are relying on drugs, some on sex, and others on buying some new thing to lift their spirits. Those who have traced the outcome of these options know they are life-destroying rather than life-building. Jesus said the principle for personal renewal, vitality, and hope is to "repent, and believe in the gospel." He said, "The time is fulfilled." Now's the time. The time is right. The reality of an ultimate Presence, potential purpose, and power are immediately available. The way to be renewed in this love and power is the same as it was the first day Jesus called men to be His disciples. It is through repenting and believing in the Gospel. The initial step into the Christian life is an act of the will involving commitment (repentance), confidence (belief), and confession (honesty with God, ourselves, and others).

1. First, we enter the Christian life by an act of *commitment.* When Joshua led his people into Canaan he said, "Choose this day whom you will serve . . ." Joshua (24:15). We know that when we make a commitment in marriage, we give ourselves. The Christian is one who unconditionally gives himself to Christ. The following is the prayer some of us have found essential for beginning each day: "Grant me the grace this day to surrender myself without reservation to the Lordship of Jesus Christ and to know the guidance and strength of the Holy Spirit."

The Bible gives a promise of what happens when this commitment is made. "Therefore, if any one is in Christ, he is a new creation; the old has passed away, behold, the new has come" (2 Corinthians 5:17). Here is the principle, promise, and power for renewal. Commitment is repentance, repentance is turning from self to Christ. The Christian is one who finds his life renewed from within by Christ.

Once I thought the hardest thing in the world was to ask a girl for a date. That's simple compared to overcoming the egocentric drive in myself to bend, twist, and turn everything to please myself. However, no matter how clever, successful, or persuasive I am in such manipulating I remain strangely uneasy and dissatisfied. I remain egocentric and empty until I allow Christ to take over at the center of my life. Paul said, "I have been crucified with Christ; it is no longer I who live, but Christ who lives in me . . ." (Galatians 2:20). Jesus said, ". . . Except a man be born again, he cannot see the kingdom of God" (John 3:3 KJV). Only as I die to self and come alive again in Christ will I discover the dominion of God's rule and power in my life. Jesus said, "If any man would come after me, let him deny himself and take up his cross daily and follow me" (Luke 9:23).

Recently a young couple called from a distant city. When they first attended worship with us at Covenant a few years ago they were discouraged, confused, and unhappy with each other. He was finishing a Ph.D. degree in biological sciences. I will never forget their dismal, antagonistic attitude the first time I called on them about two years ago.

After some time this couple joined the "Way of Life" study series in which we discuss the basic principles of the Christian life much as we are doing in these chapters. When that series concluded they continued in a small group. Within that intimate fellowship they struggled with the intellectual problems plaguing them and they poured out their deepest antagonisms and hurts. They found the answers of the biblical faith, the cleansing power of Christ's love, and the power of His Spirit. They found new life.

Joe finished his studies at Purdue University and took a job with a large corporation in New York where he and Sally started looking around immediately for Christian fellowship. When they found that the congregations they visited were lifeless, they wrote and asked me what to do. I encouraged them to prayerfully trust God to lead them to people where they were needed. They found a struggling congregation with a new pastor who was open and searching. He was aware of the urgent needs in the lives of people and in his own life for which he had nothing to offer. Sally and Joe shared with him what had happened in their lives and he was eager to hear more.

The recent phone call from this couple was to express their amazement and joy. The session of their new church had asked them to lead a "Way of Life" series. Five couples had indicated the desire to be in the first group. God has established a center from which new life will begin to awaken throughout that congregation. Meaning and hope have begun to fill empty, despairing lives. They have discovered the principle of renewal. The time is right! The Kingdom of God is at hand. First, new life comes through commitment, an act of surrender, an act of repentance in which we turn from self to Christ.

2. Second, we enter new life through an act of *confidence.* This is the step of trust, faith, or belief. ". . . the life I now live in the flesh I live by faith in the Son of God, who loved me and gave himself for me" (Galatians 2:20). We enter the Christian life by a deliberate act

of our will. We transfer our trust from ourselves, from our own strength and goodness to Christ, to what He has done for us through His cross and Resurrection and to what He seeks to do in our lives at this moment.

This all began to open up for me a few years ago when a group of three people began meeting on Wednesday evening to pray. The spark of renewal which has brought new life to me and to our whole congregation began in this group. When they informed me that they were meeting, I explained that I just would not be able to be with them because I was too busy. They said, "We understand and that is all right. We are praying that God will sustain you with His love and power in all you are doing." I was grateful, I needed all the help I could get.

A short time later I began to be aware of new strength and peace in my tense and hectic life. I knew this had come to me through the prayers of these people. Soon I joined them and found deeper and deeper evidences of God's love renewing my life in many dimensions. I knew that whatever standing I have before God, whatever strength I possess, is not on the basis of my own goodness or ability but is only through what Christ does for me bringing me into a closer relationship with God, filling me with the power of God.

The word *faith* and the words *to believe* are the same word in the New Testament. These words mean to trust or to have confidence. We enter the Christian life by an act of faith when we believe the Good News of Christ, when we trust what He has done for us and what He can do in our lives.

Mark gives us this interesting portrait of Jesus when He is calling His disciples. He comes along the lake. Peter and Andrew, James and John are fishing. He says, "Follow me!" They leave their nets and follow Him (*see* Mark 1:16-20). It all seems rather abrupt to us. We speculate that they may have heard of Christ's coming, that an urgent longing existed within them, and that He spoke deeply to their dilemma. Whatever was the case, the important fact is that Christ bore a claim within Himself upon their lives. They could trust Him.

He awakened their confidence. They followed Him discovering new life. First, this new life is discovered through commitment and second, through confidence or trust.

3. Third, we enter the Christian life through an act of *confession*. The act of confession is primarily an honest expression or disclosure of what is most deeply within ourselves. It means literally to agree with God about what is actually within us. It is an inventory of the thoughts and feelings which are dominating our lives. So we may confess our faith, our sin, our doubt, our fear, our pride.

Many of us who consider ourselves Christians are not experiencing the victories and joys that supposedly go with this life. Many of us cannot understand why we continue to get angry, fearful, or depressed. We simply plunge into the depths of anxiety or hostility and feel intensely guilty about it. Renewal comes in confessing these deepest hurts to a group of trusted Christians and relying upon God's forgiving love rather than fretting over our own weaknesses (*see* James 5:16).

Confession is the act of opening our soul to God and letting Him cleanse and fill our soul with the power of His love. Once we can actually give up all that is within us to God, we will experience a renewal mightier than the dawn, just as the darkness of the night gives way to the light of a new day. With confession there is room for God and new life in our lives. "If we confess our sins, he is faithful and just, and will forgive our sins and cleanse us from all unrighteousness" (1 John 1:9).

My wife Vivian and I experienced the reality of confession and a cleansed life at Explo 72. We were in Dallas with one hundred thousand "turned-on" young people. But there was strain and tension in our lives which was intensely distressing. We were seeking a deep renewal. We were tempted to rush all over the city to hear famous speakers. Rather we prayed, "Lord, we trust ourselves to You. You have something You want to do with us. Put us where You want us."

Our assignment card indicated we were in a group of five hundred people who were taking the basic class. How far down the line does a pastor have to start? I thought I knew something. Then I learned

24

our leader was Dr. Ralph E. Walls, a dentist from Indianapolis. Why did I come one thousand miles to Dallas to hear a dentist who lives sixty miles away from us?

Then Dr. Walls introduced us to this concept of confession. We discovered the secret of a cleansed life as we experienced God's love and forgiveness. Quietly and openly we considered what was most deeply within our lives—hurt, jealousy, envy, pride, thoughts, habits, and motives which were not healthy. These were surrendered, confessed to God. Now there was room for His love to fill, cleanse, heal, and transform us.

We prayed for His love to fill the void created by our surrender of worry and anger. We expected to receive this love. We trusted His promise of forgiveness. We began to walk renewed and refreshed, confident of what He would continue to accomplish in our lives through faith. The deep renewal we were seeking had become a reality in our experience as the strain and stress were lifted from our lives and we were filled with the cleansing, restoring love of Christ.

2

The Principle of a Spirit-Filled Life

. . . this is he who baptizes with the Holy Spirit.

John 1:33

We are focusing our attention on the person of Jesus Christ as portrayed in the four Gospels of the New Testament. We are discussing the six principles He gives as the basis for the Christian life. These are His action plan for bringing life and hope to our lives. We have discussed how we appropriate new life in Christ through commitment, confidence, and confession. Our new life in Christ is confirmed and sustained by the power of the Holy Spirit. In this chapter we are discussing the principle of a Spirit-filled life. What do we mean by "Spirit-filled life"?

When I was in the eighth grade, basketball became my chief interest for eight years. Waukegan High School, which I was entering the next fall, had not won a Suburban League game for a long time. The new coach contacted every eighth-grade basketball player personally and put us into a summer park-and-recreation program where we were introduced to what were then some sophisticated elements of the fast break, full-court press, and one-handed jump shot. He offered a basket and backboard free to any boy who would agree to mount it ten feet above the ground. By fall we were a basketball city. Spirit had come alive and continued to build. We were a spirit-filled school. That year we won the Suburban League and in three years we were number one in the state.

We know spirit is important to a team, a school, and a nation. If we can speak of team spirit, national spirit, and the characteristic spirit of a man, it is completely logical that we should speak of the

26

Spirit of God. We can also logically speak of God's Spirit as the Holy Spirit just as we speak of His Holy Word. The Word and the Spirit of God are holy and sacred. So also the Holy Spirit of God is infinite in power and just as capable of filling our lives as team spirit or school spirit. Jesus said, "You shall receive power when the Holy Spirit has come upon you . . ." (Acts 1:8). You shall have a Spirit-filled life.

People are discovering this dynamic spiritual force. A radiant, responsible Spirit has come into the lives of many young people and is evident even to their parents. Many adults are finding the joy of a Spirit-filled life and their children are saying, "Hey, that's neat! Mom and Dad are turning on to God!" How do we live a Spirit-filled life?

1. First, the Spirit of God enters our lives when this is our chief *expectation.* The Bible teaches that when we ask Christ into our lives by faith we can expect to receive the Holy Spirit because the Spirit Christ gives is the Holy Spirit. God has bestowed on Christ the Holy Spirit, who is the Spirit of Christ, the same Spirit whom Christ offers to us.

The four Gospels give us the portrait of Christ when He comes to the river Jordan where John is baptizing many people. John recognizes Christ and says, "Behold, the Lamb of God, who takes away the sin of the world!" (John 1:29). According to Matthew and Mark, Christ is baptized, and according to all four Gospels, the Holy Spirit descends upon Him. This is not the first time the Holy Spirit has acted in Christ's life in a unique way. It was announced to Mary, "The Holy Spirit will come upon you . . . therefore the child to be born will be called holy . . ." (Luke 1:35).

Christ is baptized at the river Jordan and the Holy Spirit descends upon Him commissioning and confirming the work to which He is called upon this earth. (The coming of the Holy Spirit upon Christ will not be interpreted in the adoptionist manner if John 1 and Philippians 2 are taken seriously.) John the Baptist, looking at Christ, says, ". . . This is he who baptizes with the Holy Spirit" (John 1:33). The wording here indicates that this is Christ's unique and distinctive work. So, according to John 1:29 and John 1:33, when we ask Christ

27

to come into our lives, two things happen. First, He cleanses our lives from all sin ("Behold, the Lamb of God, who takes away the sin. . . ."). Second, He fills our lives with the Holy Spirit ("This is he who baptizes with the Holy Spirit"). Christ takes away our sins and gives the Holy Spirit.

On the day of Pentecost, Peter and the rest of the disciples received the Holy Spirit. Peter proclaimed the Gospel. Those who heard asked, "Brethren, what shall we do?" and Peter said to them, "Repent, and be baptized every one of you in the name of Jesus Christ for the forgiveness of your sins; and you shall receive the gift of the Holy Spirit" (Acts 2:38).

When we repent, that is, turn from self to Christ in an act of commitment or surrender, when we believe the Gospel, that is, trust what Christ does for us through His redeeming love upon the cross, we may expect Christ to be within us in the full power of His Spirit, the Holy Spirit.

Many people consider themselves Christians and have made a personal commitment to Christ but are simply without the power and the vitality which have been promised to us in the Christian life. Many of us feel deeply guilty because tension, inner conflict, and impatience continue to plague us. The first step toward realizing the presence of the Holy Spirit within us is expectation.

2. The second step is to *desire* the presence of the Holy Spirit within us. For how many of us was our last thought before sleep and our first thought upon awakening this morning the desire to live the Spirit-filled life? But, Jim, why morning and night do you have to expect and desire to be filled with the Spirit? That's simple, I leak! My spiritual bucket gets tipped over rather easily and I allow all sorts of unhealthy, ungodly influences to possess me (evil spirits, the spirit of envy, covetousness, jealousy, and fear can utterly consume me). What is my chief desire and expectation?

There are two important concepts in the biblical faith. One is God's command and the second is God's promise. In Ephesians 5:18 God commands us, "Be filled with the Spirit" (not wine). Here we have God's command. In First John 5:14,15 we have His promise by which this command can be realized: ". . . if we ask anything according to his will he hears us. And if we know that he hears us in whatever we ask, we know that we have obtained the requests made of him."

This is His promise, when we ask according to His will, we have obtained the request. His will, His command is that we be filled with the Spirit. When this is our prayer, our expectation, and our desire, we can live in the confidence (trusting by faith) that He will keep His promise granting the power and vitality of His Spirit within us. We discover the reality of a Spirit-filled life primarily by trusting the Word of God's promise.

As Christians we live in a two-fold confidence. First, when we ask Christ by faith to come into our lives we will receive the Holy Spirit, for this is His Spirit, the Spirit He bestows upon us. Second, when our expectation is according to God's command to be filled with the Spirit He will keep His promise and answer the request which is according to His will.

One night a few years ago, when I was discovering the reality of a Christ-centered life, I found other influences besetting me and I couldn't sleep. Instead of watching Johnny Carson or "the Late Late Show" I read the New Testament. Then I knelt before the large window in our living room. The moon was flooding the whole earth with light and I knew that in a similar way God can flood the inner depths of our lives with His Spirit when our desire and expectation are upon Him.

A young couple was at Purdue University a few years ago. Carl was working toward an advanced industrial-management degree. He had managed to complete an arduous course of study, but his marriage was a shambles. He asked me to help him understand the mess. I listened for quite a while to all the gruesome details. I said, "Carl, will you allow me to take the direct approach?"

He replied, "I need it!" I explained how the Bible teaches that a new life, a Spirit-filled life can become ours. He asked Christ to come into his life by faith and experienced the joy and strength of this conviction. But suddenly he said, "What about Joan? She won't even talk about our marriage and is completely antagonistic toward God."

I said, "Carl, let's start right now to trust the Lord in all things. We will pray that God will win Joan to Himself."

Carl went back to their home and before he had his coat off Joan said, "Carl, I think we'd better talk about our marriage." He was stunned! She hadn't spoken to him for weeks. He was experiencing the work of the Holy Spirit in answer to prayer. She said, "I don't know what I'm going to do. I'm just torn up inside."

Carl shared with her what had just happened in his life through faith in Christ. God so confirmed to Carl's mind and heart the Gospel message I had shared with him that he was able to clearly express that message point by point to his wife.

When Carl left my study I had given him two books. Joan stayed up all night and read them. When Carl awoke the next morning she prayed with him to receive Christ. That night they shared with our Wednesday evening Prayer-and-Praise Group what God had done in their lives. About three months later she shared with others concerning her gratitude for the new life God had given her.

God had used me to lead Carl to Christ on a one-to-one basis. It was only a short time before that I had learned to share my faith. This was the first time God had ever used me in this way. Carl and Joan had a new life in Christ. As we will discuss in the next chapter, that new life must mature through spiritual growth.

Carl accepted an excellent job offer in a distant city and had to go to work before their new home would be ready. It was some time before Joan and their young children could join him. He entered a small Bible-and-prayer group and grew strong in his faith. Joan went back to her home and had no spiritual fellowship. She did not grow spiritually; she became spiritually weak and fell into unhealthy practices. Carl came to see her just long enough for Joan to tell him that she never wanted to see him again.

Carl went back to his job where he supervised many workers. There was also the shattering worry for his wife and two small children. He wrote me that the pressure would have completely broken him if he had not learned to trust God by faith. Many harsh and overwhelming events followed during the next two years. While Carl and Joan were separated, a person some distance away, for a reason accountable only to the working of the Holy Spirit in the answer to prayer, sought out Joan and invited her to join a group of Spirit-filled Christians. The new life that had flickered for a time in her came to full fruition. Carl had a joyful return to a loving and faithful wife and to a Spirit-filled home.

3

The Principle of Spiritual Growth

So Jesus grew both tall and wise, and was loved by God and man.

Luke 2:52 LB

. . . attain to the . . . measure of the stature of the fulness of Christ. . . . grow up in every way into him who is the head, into Christ.

Ephesians 4:13,15

We have considered the principles of renewal and of the Spirit-filled life. We have seen that according to the biblical faith we enter the Christian life by trusting Christ to take away our sins and to fill us with the power of His Holy Spirit. When we open our lives to Christ we become a new person, we come under new management, we begin a new life. It is critical that this new life in Christ grow and mature.

Paul says the goal of such growth is to attain the full stature of Christ, growing up in every way unto Him (*see* Ephesians 4:13,15). Luke gives us the magnificent portrait of the lad Jesus: "And Jesus grew up, both in body and in wisdom, gaining favor with God and men" (Luke 2:52 TEV). This same description is given in the Old Testament concerning the lad Samuel who became the judge and prophet of Israel (*see* 1 Samuel 2:26).

1. The first step of growth in the Christian life is *discipleship*. A Christian disciple is one who is growing in his relationship to Christ. The root of the word *discipleship* is discipline. Many of us become tense when we hear the word *discipline*.

When a baby is born we know his life must grow, develop, and mature. If that new life fails to grow it will deteriorate and perish.

This growth is dependent upon proper food. The baby will receive proper food only as his diet is carefully disciplined. We don't want him eating just anything he picks up off the floor or in the dirt or that happens to be available. Discipline is essential to healthy growth.

Recently a Covenant Samaritan went into a dilapidated house near the Wabash River. There were a number of problems needing attention. The stench was unbearable. Suddenly the caller realized that there in a pile of filth was a pathetic, emaciated, starving baby. The baby was two months old, had scarcely grown six ounces since birth, and was at the point of death. The mother had been attempting to exist and to nurse her baby while eating only french fries and soda. It won't work. The baby and the mother are now being properly fed. Growth and life are dependent upon proper food.

It is equally essential that our new life in Christ grow, develop, and mature. This new life is dependent upon proper spiritual food. We will receive proper spiritual food only through discipline. Discipline is essential to spiritual growth.

The discipline Jesus encourages us to exercise is the discipline He lived out with His disciples. First, we see Him going apart to pray. He observed the practice of quiet time (*see* Mark 1:35). Second, He engaged in the discipline of group life. One of the first things He did was to form a small group. He gathered twelve disciples about Him (*see* Mark 1:16-20). People at Covenant know how convinced I am that continuing, consistent growth in the Christian life is impossible apart from a group experience. This group includes sharing in the Word and in prayer and bearing each other's burdens. Third, Jesus allowed the Word of God in Scripture to become utterly a part of His life (*see* Luke 4:17). Finally, He sought to strengthen the weak and encourage the fainthearted (*see* Luke 4:18). This discipline in which Jesus encourages us as His disciples is essential to Christian growth. He said, "If any man would come after me, let him deny himself and take up his cross daily and follow me" (Luke 9:23).

Who finds this spiritual discipline difficult? I do! It has never been natural or easy for me. The busier we become at the office, in homemaking, or in schoolwork the more difficult it is to keep this discipline and the more dependent we are upon it. The new life and vitality evident in our congregation and in countless individual lives is an inspiration. This new faith will be challenged by every extreme and unbalanced influence and it will be choked out by other cares and interests unless we put down roots deeply into the resources of God's Word, love, and power allowing this force to sustain, strengthen, and mature our faith. In chapter 1 we have discussed how the Christian life begins with an act of decision. Now we are considering how this new life in Christ grows and matures through discipline.

A couple has gone through intense strain and struggle during the past three years. He has had a serious illness which has been a horrifying ordeal. His wife came to me out of sheer desperation two months ago. Her husband had been a church member but he never expected the Christian faith to have any practical relevance in his life. Now he had become antagonistic toward God and people.

About a month ago it became evident that Peter had been healed. He has a keen and brilliant mind. But suddenly he realized he was not ready to live. The thought of living can be more terrifying than the thought of dying. Peter expressed his desperation to a friend in another city. "I've got to find something to get ahold of. Now most of our problems seem solved and we have about everything we could want since I receive full disability insurance. But my wife is on the verge of a nervous breakdown and I have nothing to live for."

The friend shared his own personal faith with Peter and told how prayer is an essential part of his life. Then he asked, "Isn't there someone in Lafayette you can talk to about your faith?"

Peter answered, "Well, there is that minister my wife has gone to talk to. When I heard he was coming by the house to visit I got out of there before he arrived."

As soon as Peter arrived home he called me. We met that day. I shared with him how a person can enter the Christian life by trusting what Christ seeks to do in his life. Peter prayed to receive Christ and he experienced new life and joy. The next morning when I arrived at the office, Peter and his wife Karin were waiting for me. The two of them prayed for guidance to walk together by faith in the Christian life.

Peter said, "We want to join one of these groups we hear so much about." Another man, a big, strong man who is a famous athlete, had sat in that same room a few months before and had made the same decision to enter the Christian life. I called him and he came by immediately to meet Peter, to welcome him into the Christian life, to invite him to meet with a group of Christian businessmen every Saturday morning, and to invite Peter and Karin to join a group of Christian couples who meet for prayer and Bible study every week. Peter and Karin have found new life in Christ and they are growing in that new life.

2. The second step of spiritual growth is *determination.* This simply means that what I have decided to do in Christian discipline, I determine to get done. Paul says:

> One thing I do. . . . I run straight toward the goal . . . which is God's call through Christ Jesus. . . . All of us who are spiritually mature should have this same attitude. If, however, some of you have a different attitude, God will make this clear to you.
>
> Philippians 3:13-15 TEV

Determination in discipline is essential whether one is losing weight or learning French. I made a New Year's resolution for physical and spiritual discipline. This discipline is simply twenty minutes' quiet time in the morning and twenty minutes' running in the evening. There is nothing impressive about this discipline, but I know my spiritual and physical health depend upon it and I am determined to keep it.

Jesus said, "By this all men will know that you are my disciples, if you have love for one another" (John 13:35). Sometimes I just don't feel very loving. Neither do I always bear the other marks of a Christian such as joy and peace (*see* Colossians 3:12-17; Galatians 5:22, 23). We are talking about determination in spiritual growth. The key step for me was *desperation.*

A few years ago the joy of a Christ-centered life had begun to flood my experience. But there was still enough of the old man left to keep

35

me under a deep sense of guilt and uncertainty. I thought Christians were not supposed to have anxiety, anger, or despair. But I did and I still do. I realized that it was critically urgent for me to grow consistently in the Christian life. It is often difficult to find the group of people with whom such continuing growth can occur. Finally, Charlie Green and Bob DeHaan, the two Navigator leaders on the Purdue campus, offered to meet with me weekly in a time of Bible study, prayer, and fellowship. Here in this Christian fellowship were the ingredients for personal growth. I have discovered in William Parker's book *Prayer Can Change Your Life* a pattern for personal quiet time which has made this practice the most essential period of each day and strategic to personal effectiveness.

3. Spiritual growth involves discipline and determination. It comes through desperation for some of us. Finally, vital spiritual growth involves a deep sense of *dependence*. It is God who is ultimately in charge of our growth, who finally brings the increase (*see* 1 Thessalonians 3:12,13). Some of us may come to desire spiritual growth out of desperation. We just have to learn the hard way that life is going to become empty, meaningless, and desperate apart from a close walk with God. But finally spiritual growth occurs when I relax in deep, humble, quiet trust and dependence upon God, confident of what He will do in my life. Then I enter times of prayer, engage in biblical living, and join in Christian fellowship not out of duty, determination, or desperation, but out of a deep sense of expectation concerning what God is seeking to accomplish in my life and through me in the lives of others.

4

The Principle of Compassion
—Samaritans

But a Samaritan, as he journeyed, came to where he was; and when
he saw him, he had compassion, and went to him and bound up
his wounds . . . and took care of him.

Luke 10:33,34

Christ makes it abundantly clear that there are two crucial dimensions to the life He offers: conviction and compassion. To maintain a vital balance between conviction and compassion is essential in a healthy Christian life. Elton Trueblood is fond of saying that the holy conjunction is the word *and*. So we have conviction and compassion summarizing the Christian imperative.

People are inclined to take one aspect of the Christian life and run off with it, ignoring its balancing counterpart. We have seen how conviction without compassion becomes harsh, narrow, belligerent, bigoted, and insensitive. Compassion without a sustaining center of conviction becomes easily disillusioned and resentful. In the principles we have already discussed we have summarized the very heart of Christian conviction. Now we are concerned with the heart of Christian compassion.

In Luke 10 we find a lawyer testing Jesus on His qualifications as a teacher. Jesus turns a question back to the lawyer, who summarizes the entire Old Testament law precisely as Jesus does in Matthew 22:34-39. They both give the same two-fold summary with "and" in the middle. First, Deuteronomy 6:4 is the summary concerning conviction. "You shall love the Lord your God with all your heart, and with all your soul, and with all your might." And second, from Leviticus 19:18 the summary of compassion is given: "You shall love your neighbor as yourself. . . ."

The lawyer seems to sense that Jesus finds a fuller meaning in Leviticus 19:18 than had previously been understood. This is precisely what Jesus does. He is answering the question, "Who is my neighbor?" The answer He gives with the parable of the Good Samaritan is startling and revolutionary. The Jew considered his neighbor to be other Jews. He did not consider a person of another nationality his neighbor. Jesus gives the startling word that our neighbor is anyone who is in need. Compassion is spontaneous, sacrificial love for anyone who is suffering. Such compassion is the unique and distinctive quality of the Christian life: "They'll know we are Christians by our love."

1. First of all, according to this parable Christian love for others, compassion, is *spontaneous.* A man of the Jews was robbed, beaten, and left half-dead beside the road. Even the most religious of his own people were indifferent as they hurried past.

A Samaritan came that way. The most intense antagonism existed between the Samaritans and the Jews. It was the sort of deep, complex bitterness between two people or groups of people such as causes a Catholic and a Protestant in Ireland to be engaged in a death struggle, and a black or white person in this country to keep certain fears and hates alive.

The Samaritan saw the desperate plight of the wounded Jew. The Samaritan was sensitive to the suffering of his enemy. He was moved with compassion and spontaneously attended to the needs of his enemy without regard for whether or not the injured man deserved such help. He took no thought of what this enemy would do to him in a similar circumstance. He didn't consider how careless this man had been, nor was he deterred by the fact that the man's own people wouldn't help. He took no thought of return. He didn't rely upon welfare to take care of a person who was in difficulty. He simply helped the man who was in need spontaneously. Jesus said, "Go and do likewise" (Luke 10:37).

The life of compassion to which Christ calls us is a life of spontaneous concern for a person who is in need, without consideration for whether he deserves such help, whether he will appreciate it, or whether the help given will be wasted. There is no thought of return, nor of the outcome. A person who suffers even because of his own folly is loved by God. He is of infinite worth in the sight of God who created him, and God entrusts him to our care. Such spontaneous, unselfish, unconditional, uncalculating love was revolutionary the day Jesus introduced it and it still is today.

Today a person is in need and destitute. What do we hear? "I made it on my own, it's up to him." "This guy is lazy." "You can't trust him." "He's no good." "Anything you do for that family is useless." "Forget it!" "No matter what you do for him it won't do any good."

Lord, when did we see You hungry and feed You, thirsty and give You drink? And when did we see You a stranger and welcome You, or naked and clothe You, and when did we see You sick or in prison and visit You? And Jesus said the Lord will answer them, "Truly, I say to you, as you did it to one of the least of these my brethren, you did it to me" (Matthew 25:40).

Compassion is the mark of a Christian. Jesus said:

A new commandment I give to you, that you love one another; even as I have loved you, that you also love one another. By this all men will know that you are my disciples, if you have love for one another.

John 13:34

Anyone within the range of our outreach who suffers has been entrusted by God to our care. The depth of our compassion for this person is a witness to our faith in Christ, the measure of our love for Him, and our gratitude for the love He pours out upon our lives.

I pray:

that Christ may dwell in your hearts through faith; that you, being rooted and grounded in love, may have power to comprehend . . .

39

the breadth and length and height and depth, and to know the love
of Christ which surpasses knowledge, that you may be filled with
all the fulness of God.

Ephesians 3:17-21

Throughout the area where each of us lives there are dependent
mothers left in hovels with children without shoes, without food,
without guidance, without hope, without anything we would consider
absolutely essential. Most of us remain oblivious to these and countless other desperate needs of people who live within three minutes of
us. Most of us are not moved with compassion to the extent of
stepping out of our busy routine to help them. "Religion that is pure
and undefiled before God and the Father is this: to visit orphans and
widows in their affliction . . ." (James 1:27). We pass by such persons
daily.

People are going out daily from Covenant into these homes, into
situations where sickness, stench, and suffering are overwhelming.
Food, clothing, heat, medical attention, and the love of Christ are
shared. We told the story in an earlier chapter of one of these visits.
Recently a caller entered a home. Nine children were jammed into
an unsafe upstairs room. They had no washer. Twelve loads of horribly dirty clothing were done at the launderette. Later we installed a
washer in the house. The children were without shoes but now they
have them. The father had no job but now he is working.

We could go on to talk of derelict and hopeless men who wander
from one sort of trouble and desperation to another. We could talk
of young people, school dropouts, who have little helpful guidance
or encouragement in finding a life that is full and healthy. Then there
are the elderly people who are alone and suffering. Human need of
the most intense sort surrounds us, waits on our doorstep for attention. The compassion Christ offers in Himself for those who are in
need is first of all spontaneous, uncalculating, unconditional.

When we organized Covenant Church in 1958 there were a few
individuals who became exceptionally capable in helping people. The

deacons formed the Fellowship of Christian Sharing. This group has sought to have the resources and ability available to respond to any form of human need, giving help with housing, food, medicine, tutoring, or transportation. A deacons' fund was established so people can give to this cause at any time. People give freely and generously. Particular needs are always met when they are made known. This group has sponsored a medical referral center, a neighborhood-development project, and an afternoon program for children and mothers.

2. Second, the compassion Christ offers in Himself as the characteristic mark of the Christian is *sacrificial.* Christian love is costly. Christ gave Himself for us. When He sees the selfish, contemptuous, undeserving condition of our lives He does not turn from us. Rather He has taken upon Himself the burden which our selfishness has caused but which we refuse to bear and are unable to bear. Christ's love for us is sacrificial.

Christ does not allow the selfishness or depravity of any life to set a limit to His self-giving. He has come into a world of sin and has given Himself upon the cross for us: "For our sake he made him to be sin who knew no sin, so that in him we might become the righteousness of God" (2 Corinthians 5:21).

Such sacrificial love gives itself completely, aware that it will be exploited, wasted, and abused. In the face of such indifference and abuse, Christ's love for us remains constant. This is the only possibility by which my unworthy life can come into fellowship with God. The love of Christ constrains us. His love is spontaneous and sacrificial. He calls us to love one another. If you believe Christ is calling you to help a person in serious need in your community, the way is open for you.

In the Fellowship of Christian Sharing we have learned that the key to helping people who are suffering is a continuing personal contact. We have come to believe that it is crucial for more Covenant members to become involved in this dimension of the Christian life. So we have developed the opportunity for families to become Samaritans. Our goal is to equip a family in Covenant to go to a family which

41

has become a victim of life and with God's help restore that family to responsible, abundant living.

This Samaritan endeavor has proved to be a strategic way to involve entire families from our congregation in a personal ministry of compassion. Eighteen families originally began this work and were soon helping families with intense and diverse problems. When the Samaritans meet for prayer and mutual encouragement it is an inspirational experience. Progress with the problems they encounter is usually painfully slow. But we are convinced that this is the most effective sort of help that can be given. The objective is to share the love of God which has filled our lives through Jesus Christ. We trust God to use these acts of love to restore life, health, and faith to those immediately around us who are suffering and whom God entrusts to our care.

The Wabash River flows between Lafayette and West Lafayette. Covenant Church is located in the residential area of West Lafayette on the bluff above the river. South of town along the river are pathetic hovels where people attempt to live. One of the shacks burned during the winter. An entire family was left destitute. Someone said to them, "Go to that church up there, they help people." We consider this the finest compliment we could receive. We know our best efforts fall short of Christ's full imperative. We continually rediscover our total dependence upon His grace.

5

The Principle of Emotional Wholeness

A kingdom divided against itself will collapse.

Mark 3:24 LB

Events which once brought tears now bring laughter to us. The emotional capacity of the human personality is rich and dramatic. When Vivian and I went to Nassau for our honeymoon, I assumed we would see the island on bicyles and she assumed it would be by taxi. The conflicting emotions aroused by these two means of transportation were all brought with us as a surprise into married life. Our relationship today is beautiful and fulfilling because we have learned how to get in touch with our feelings and how to deal with them in a constructive way. Such emotional honesty has not been easy and offers a continuing challenge.

Jesus portrays in Himself the personal wholeness we all cherish. When the mind, will, and emotions are integrated in Him, there is the awareness of becoming more and more complete as a person. People who are experiencing balanced growth in these three crucial areas of the personality speak of becoming all of one piece. We have the urgent need to find how the fragmented pieces of our lives can begin to fit together. In this chapter we are discussing emotional wholeness, which is an essential ingredient of a complete and balanced life.

Consider the emotional strain Jesus was under just from the events described in the third chapter of Mark. The Pharisees attacked Jesus for healing the withered hand of a man on the Sabbath. "And he looked around at them with anger, grieved at their hardness of heart" (3:5). "The Pharisees went out, and immediately held counsel with the Herodians against him, how to destroy him" (3:6). People pressed in upon Him wherever He went, even when He went to the sea with His disciples and when He came home (*see* 3:7-10,19,20). His own friends tried to seize Him, convinced that He was out of His mind (*see* 3:21). His mother and brothers had no understanding of what He was doing (*see* 3:31). Jesus was subject to the most intense emotional strain. This strain was felt within the depth of His life, arousing tears and anger. For all the intensity of the feelings He knew and faced His emotions were neither devisive nor harmful, but served the full purpose of His redeeming love.

It is Jesus' capacity to feel joy and sorrow and to be acquainted with our hopes and fears that makes Him real and precious to us. The emotional capacity of the human personality is rich and diverse. We are able to experience simple joy and profound inspiration, genuine happiness and deep fulfillment, playful humor and robust enjoyment. From our feelings comes the force for creative genius, life-restoring compassion, and life-sustaining affection. The Psalms of the Old Testament portray the deepest and most vital emotions of the human heart: peace, love, joy, hope, trust, gratitude, and satisfaction. These emotions fill, sustain, strengthen, and fulfill the human soul.

The Psalms also portray forceful emotions which bring strain and stress to the inner life: fear, hate, guilt, sorrow, indignation, and terror. These emotions can have a constructive influence. The fear aroused within us when a child is in danger may stimulate the action necessary to provide for his well-being. These feelings may also be kept bottled up within until we break emotionally from the strain. Recognizing and dealing constructively with our deepest feelings is essential to becoming a whole person.

We are taught to hide and repress our feelings and some of us are conditioned against allowing ourselves to have any feeling. We tell our sons at an early age that big boys don't cry (even though Jesus wept). We want to be sure people see us as strong, radiant, confident people. This means that many distressing feelings have to be held in and kept to ourselves. Feelings of doubt and despair arise within us. Everyone else seems so controlled and self-confident that we find no way to share our deepest needs and we live a lonely existence. Emotional control is vital for channeling our energy into constructive endeavor. Emotional repression can leave our inner life torn to pieces by unresolved emotions.

At a very early age emotional hurts and weaknesses arise within our deepest self. None of us can ever have all of our emotional needs met. The unresolved conflicts are so painful that we deal with them by pushing them out of our mind, but they never leave us. They are left at a subconscious level and require the major portion of our psychic energy to keep them out of sight.

The strain of these unresolved fears and hates surfaces in the form of countless symptoms such as backaches and headaches, depression, and compulsive activity. We may take aspirin for our headache and a drink for depression, but we are dealing only with the symptom, not the repressed fear or hostility which causes the symptom. Learning how to identify and resolve our deepest feelings is essential to becoming a whole person. The following are the three essential steps to becoming emotionally whole.

1. *Become emotionally honest with God, self, and others.* Emotional strength arises when I can honestly say, "This I am and this I will become." The extent to which we face the truth of our liabilities and potentialities is the extent to which we will experience victory or defeat. Each of us has emotional weakness and emotional strength which as yet remain unidentified. The means God has offered to us for becoming emotionally honest and strong is confession. This act of confession involves honesty with ourselves, with God, and with others. When we experience Christian fellowship in a small group where trust and acceptance have been established (*see* James 5:16), we will find the encouragement to bring the deepest areas of our lives confidently, clearly before the redeeming, restoring love of Christ.

Many who consider themselves Christians feel guilty and distressed when they continue to experience depression, fear, or doubt. Paul, the dynamic apostle, in the midst of his Christian life cried out, "I do not understand my own actions . . ." (Romans 7:15). Here is evidence of a divided, hidden self, a force within which was working against his becoming a whole person, a force which he saw Christ alone having the power to resolve (*see* Romans 7:24). It is at this subconscious level that we see Paul experiencing conflict and being drawn into actions which are distressing and difficult to understand. We see Paul again and again seeking through honest confession to bring the fragmented pieces of his inner life under the restoring power of Christ's love. The first step to emotional wholeness is to become emotionally honest with ourselves, with God, and with others, as an attitude of trust, acceptance, and mutual encouragement is being built.

2. *Surrender all unhealthy attitudes and feelings.* When we recognize deep inner fear, guilt, or hostility we can allow Christ to accept these burdens upon Himself and to take them from our lives. To continue to dwell on a hidden fear or repressed hostility once we have clearly recognized its presence is to hold it to ourselves rather than giving it to the One who alone can free us from this inner enemy. Jesus reminds us that a house, a life, a marriage divided against itself cannot stand. He seeks to restore inner unity and peace within the depths of our lives. "If we confess our sins, he is faithful and just, and will forgive our sins and cleanse us from all unrighteousness" (1 John 1:9).

As we face problems and troubles which can arouse incapacitating fear or anxiety, we now understand the emotional weakness within ourselves from which these negative emotions arise when aggravated by some difficulty. We consciously surrender the feelings and the problem, refusing to concentrate upon them, confident that Christ will accept this burden. We define our problem as precisely as possible, we seek the best solution and live out the answer. When worry and fear come back we do not harbor them. Rather we hold a positive image of ourselves, of our abilities, and of the solution to our problem. In this pattern we will move from victory to victory rather than from defeat to defeat.

3. *Receive God's love and power into the depths of life.* We may identify a negative emotion or attitude warring within us and we may be able to surrender this guilt or fear to God but we must develop the capacity to receive the restoring, sustaining love of Christ into the

inner depths of our lives or we will become possessed by another spirit perhaps even worse than the first (*see* Matthew 12:43-45). At definite times of prayer each day ask God to fill the inner depths of your life with His love. Meditate on the wonder of God's love. Allow the power of His love to touch, fill, and condition the depths of your being. Maintain positive images of the self His love enables you to realize. "God shows his love for us in that while we were yet sinners Christ died for us" (Romans 5:8).

Our inner life will become filled with the power of God's love, first, when we become deeply aware of His love for us and second, when we allow our love for God to grow. Love God with all your heart, soul, mind, and strength (*see* Mark 12:30). We become whole when we love God wholly and heartily. Third, love others even as you have become able to love and respect yourself through God's love (*see* Mark 12:31). Our feelings may still be lagging; someone may still arouse deep resentment. Do the loving thing and allow feelings to catch up with a loving act. Finally, consider the love of others for you. No matter how faint, there are those who care what happens to you. Let this glimmer of love blossom in the depths of your life.

A young man named Mike had absorbed intense emotional conflict from his parents. When he informed his parents that he was going to drop out of college his father told him he would have to move out of the house. This confirmed a deep feeling of rejection Mike had always felt. The feeling of fear filled his inner life. As I was able to help him realize that this was a fear of being rejected and of failure, he began to understand why school had been so difficult. As he took the step of becoming emotionally honest with himself and with God he was able to accept himself, understanding the inner war that had virtually consumed him. When he consciously surrendered all hate and fear from his life he became free to discover the wholesome, positive qualities which could become a reality in his life.

For the first time Mike became aware of the amazing depths of God's love for him. He was free to believe and doubt not. He was able to respect himself and believe in his capacity for achievement and love. From this perspective he recognized the emotional distress consuming his parents. He was able to accept them without trying to change them. He was able to do the loving thing even when his feelings were holding back. He has come to know Christ in a personal way, understanding the meaning of His cross and suffering. Mike has become an agent of Christ's love in the world.

6

The Principle of Intellectual Wholeness

Why are you afraid, O men of little faith?

Matthew 8:26

Jesus uses keen, probing questions to reach the very center of a man's awareness. This is not a game. He is calling with compelling force for intellectual integrity concerning the basic motives of our lives. He recognizes that the consuming fears possessing us are but the consequence of presuppositions which are not adequate to sustain life. He asks the difficult questions which force us to turn the full light of reason upon the presuppositions by which we live and to face up to their outcome.

How do we best show the intellectual integrity of the Christian faith? How do we help the world see that Christianity is not based upon blind faith but is based upon the only rational answer to the most pressing questions of human life? How shall we make it clear that Christianity is not just one of many possibilities but is the only alternative to futility?

1. First of all, the validity of the Christian answer is set forth in its fullest strength when we are prepared to *move from a defensive to an offensive position.* Jesus asked the keen, cutting questions which reach to the center of a man's awareness and compel him to be intellectually honest about the consequences of the presuppositions by which he is living. Let's bring the full light of reason upon the dilemmas of contemporary life and find out why we are under such stress. "Why are you afraid, O men of little faith?"

This probing and challenging of men until they are compelled to face up to the tumultuous condition of their inner lives must take place in the full context of life. Jesus was out where people were living. He was helping those who were in distress. He was a part of the human scene. From within that situation he gently and forcefully invited men to examine the goals of their lives, where they placed their trust, what actually were the convictions by which they lived, and what they could reasonably expect to follow.

The mood of our time is characterized by restless searching as people remain disturbed and doubtful. We are faced with a crisis of conscience and conviction. Men are not really sure what they believe or how to maintain integrity. Rationalism has attempted to start with man and, without any other point of reference, to unfold the full meaning of life in a closed system. We must continually remind our contemporaries of the consequences of such man-centered rationalism, showing the tragic despair filling the lives of even our most prominent contemporaries who refuse to open their minds to a fuller dimension of reality than exists within themselves. We refute rationalism but insist upon being fully rational, which means using the full light of reason to be clear about what is and what is not true to life.

Man is the only creature who remains harassed of soul, uneasy of conscience, and distressed of mind, even when provided with every physical necessity. He alone can ask questions about his inner uneasiness. He is able to ask for he is separated from, while participating in, what he is asking about. In the midst of the tragic sense of despair, we hear reports of men finding direction and hope to which they manage to hold even in the face of intense difficulty. They maintain a certain confidence and expectation about life's final worth and meaning. Inevitably they will affirm that their minds have been awakened by Christ and He has given total confidence about tomorrow. Why do we possess a tragic sense of futility and a moral uneasiness? It is because we have been created for a purpose, and we are under a moral imperative from an urgent and gracious Presence who has fashioned our existence and created a destiny for us.

First of all, a Christian will demonstrate the validity of the Christian faith when he takes the offensive and asks the difficult questions about the contemporary sense of tragedy and moral uneasiness.

2. Second, the Christian will demonstrate the validity of the Chris-

tian faith when he is able to *offer the Christian answer,* when he shows that Christianity is not based on a blind leap of faith but upon the only rational answer to the most pressing questions of human existence. Paul said, "We destroy arguments and every proud obstacle to the knowledge of God, and take every thought captive to obey Christ" (2 Corinthians 10:5).

Let's ask one of the difficult questions of life and consider the Christian answer. "Why can a man be so noble at one time and so treacherous at another?" How can men sense the infinite worth of human life and still be dominated by such a tragic sense of despair? Ask yourself, ask history, ask philosophy, ask religion, ask the Scriptures. After you have a thousand answers see which one holds up before the evidence.

Stand in the Cathedral of Amiens, where the Gothic nave rises 140 feet in magnificent splendor and you sense the nobility of the human spirit. Go to that little Mount Canaan Sunday school early on Sunday morning with David Rule down in the Appalachian Mountains near Stanton, Kentucky, and you will see the joy, the hope, and the incentive for living being brought into the lives of these people. You will be encountering the nobility of the human spirit which caused the psalmist to exclaim:

> O Lord our Lord, how excellent is thy name in all the earth! . . .
> What is man, that thou art mindful of him? . . . For thou hast made
> him a little lower than the angels, and hast crowned him with glory
> and honour.

> Psalms 8:1,4,5 KJV

Then go to Buchenwald where one hundred thousand people were exterminated like insects and realize that these were but a fraction of the people disposed of in this way by the Nazi menace. And we have the overwhelming sense of tragedy we so often face as described by Jeremiah: "The heart is deceitful above all things, and desperately corrupt . . . (17:9).

Here is the dilemma of man with all his potential nobility and potential depravity. We are living among a generation of decision makers who despair of finding any escape from the futility that plagues the contemporary mind. This is why our society has a loss of confidence and a crisis of conscience. We are a despairing people and we have settled for motives which are far from noble. The tragedy of our motives is constantly being revealed. We play the game each day but at night we can scarcely sleep for the dread that stalks us. In the next ten years the crisis of conscience and the loss of confidence will mount to such magnitude that the present crisis will not even be remembered.

We can't explain man's distinctiveness and uniqueness by reducing him to the mere physical properties of the DNA structure. This sort of determinism reduces man to a machine and this is what all the young people are crying out against.

There is a personal quality to human life and to ignore this is to deny the evidence. Man is moral, he possesses a conscience and this is distinctive about him. He knows that something is wrong within himself and his relationship to others. The only possible answer is that there is a moral absolute for which the conscience of man has been created.

Man is overwhelmed by actual moral guilt and he desperately needs a solution for that guilt. Without such a resolution he will continue to live under an inescapable weight of despair. The majestic heights of Calvary loom before the lives of all men. This is not an isolated event but the one event to which the hope of every man is related. The absolute moral demand upon our lives has been met in the perfect love of Christ for us. A way has been opened for us to fellowship with a personal God. In that fellowship we can become a new creation overcoming the tragedy of our existence, claiming the dignity and worth of life as its final characteristic and certain hope.

This answer to man's dilemma is worth grasping with the full force of our intellect and bringing home its consequences for the lives of others and for our society. "Why are you afraid, O men of little faith?"

In 1948 Edith and Francis Schaeffer and their three small children left Saint Louis and went to Switzerland to write Christian education materials. They soon found an urgent need for interpreting the Christian faith to the many agnostic, searching students who wander about Europe.

In 1955, just when their work was becoming established, their permit for residence was not renewed. They had six weeks to find and buy a house to establish residence. A passage of Scripture spoke to them as God's Word: "Let us go up to the mountain of the Lord . . . that he may teach us of his ways and that we may walk in his paths . . ." (Isaiah 2:3). They had no funds and no possibility for getting a house. They trusted in a God who exists and listens to the prayers of His children, a God who can work in ways beyond anything we ask or think.

A few days before the deadline they were informed of an old chalet high in the Alps above Lausanne. What did God have for them to do in the remote village of Huémoz? Their permit was renewed, but they had to have seven thousand dollars for the down payment in two months. They have never solicited funds. They have relied upon prayer, trusting God to move those whom He wills to make His purpose possible. A matter of hours before the deadline gifts from all over the world provided exactly for the payment.

Today there is a complex of chalets on the side of that mountain with a chapel in the middle and this is the world-famous *L'Abri* Fellowship. Francis Schaeffer asks the difficult questions of contemporary man and forces him to face the consequences of his presuppositions. He offers the Christian answer which is the only answer adequate for the contemporary dilemma. He demonstrates that the biblical faith and the biblical record are reliable.

Immediately after the Schaeffers had moved into the run-down *Chalet Les Mélèzes,* students began arriving every weekend. Each of these students was confronted with the validity of the Christian faith and their enthusiasm caused many others to follow them. Schaeffer was soon holding weekly Bible studies in Lausanne, Geneva, and Milan.

A young man named John Sandri who had studied in America arrived. All he knew was that there was an American family who had something like a house party every weekend and he asked to stay. Trained in philosophy, he possessed a keen and intensely skeptical mind. Francis Schaeffer asked him to take a walk to view the magnificent *Les Dents du Midi* mountain range across the Rhône valley. Suddenly John said, "The Christian faith doesn't really have a leg to stand on intellectually, does it, Mr. Schaeffer?" Well, in the early hours of the morning those two men were still talking in that living room which has become so famous for the discussions taking place there. For the first time in his life John Sandri realized that Christianity has not only the best answer but the only answer to the essential questions of life.

That Monday morning when John left he wrote in the guest book: "My eyes have been opened to a new world in which I hope to dwell with a coming faith." Some years later John married the Schaeffers' older daughter Priscilla, and today he is one of the key leaders at *L'Abri*.

It is one of the highest privileges of a lifetime for my wife Vivian and me and our two children, Lynn and David, to have spent two months at *L'Abri*. A strong foundation of biblical truth was established for our lives. The incomparable claims of God's Word have come home to our hearts and we continue to seek the instruction of His Word daily. We have learned what it is to live as a family before the face of the Lord, sensing the wonder of His presence more immediately than any other influence. We found our lives being bound together as a family in the bond of Christ's love. We watched confused and desperate people pass from death to life as they discovered the validity of the Christian answer to their most pressing questions. We formed cherished friendships with Edith and Francis, John and Pris, and many others. We have known a deep and profound experience of Christian community founded upon biblical truth. This is the most fulfilling and complete experience open to us upon this earth.

II

A More Complete Faith
—It Works!—James

7

The Third Way

James, a servant of God and of the Lord Jesus Christ . . . .
Let steadfastness have its full effect, that you may be . . . complete,
lacking in nothing.
Be doers of the word and not hearers only. . . .

James 1:1,4,22

We are entering an era which promises to be the most dynamic in Christian history. Evidence of this is seen in the way God is raising up men and women to rebuild His Church. I have had the privilege of traveling to many parts of this country and everywhere I have found exciting things happening in the lives of Christians. Keith Miller, in his book *The Taste of New Wine,* describes the new style of vital Christian life which is awakening within the Church today. People in all walks of life, business and professional people, pastors and their families, are discovering in experience and portraying in their lives a radiant, responsible, redemptive quality of daily life. This new spirit is evident across America. The common commitment we share is in Christ as Lord and we share the confidence that His challenge is to the whole person.

Evidence of the new life flooding our midst today is seen in the host of high-school and college students who are discovering the joy and integrity of personal faith in Christ. These young people swell our congregation beyond capacity every Sunday morning. In Dallas at Explo 72 we saw thousands of these young people winning the respect and affection of an entire city. I saw the most hateful, obscene, and dangerous militant leader from a large university campus give his life to Christ and now he is bringing the love and power of God to the ills of a society he was bent upon destroying only a few months before. Adults and youth are interested in Christ Himself because of the incomparable claim and impact He has on life.

This all comes at a time when the membership of the major denominations is seriously declining, when many are exhausted with the institutional grayness and dullness of the Church. A visiting sociologist at Purdue University declared recently that the Church could be a healthy factor within society, but so far as he can see it is not a viable influence. This is a strong indictment for many denominations whose objective has been to be socially relevant.

It seems that when the Church is obsessed only with reforming society or only with winning souls, health comes neither to the society nor to the soul. The social gospel and the personal Gospel of Christ must be held in vital balance. Our conscience has been awakened to the injustice, suffering, and prejudice in our society. We have been called to social honesty. Now we are being called to honesty before the evangel of our faith and its claim for our unconditional commitment. We are realizing that compassion and conviction must be held inseparably together if the wholeness and validity of the Christian Gospel are to be realized.

Again and again we are tempted to take one important aspect of the Christian faith and neglect another, which is to distort that faith. Compassion without conviction lacks a sustaining source of inspiration and will turn into disillusionment or bitterness. Conviction without compassion lacks love and will become harsh and bigoted.

We are inclined erroneously to narrow the choice, making it a matter of selecting either compassion or conviction. If the option is to take one or the other, if either conviction or compassion is considered sufficient in itself, the Christian faith is divided and weakened. The immensely significant insight of Christ is that we are not reduced to such a choice because there is a third way, a live option, which is to hold compassion and conviction in the vital balance portrayed to us in the person of Christ, who proclaimed repentance and practiced love. Jesus refused to settle for alternatives which were only partially valid. It was difficult but He held out for the whole and responsible way, which is to seek a vibrant personal faith that becomes evident in works. James encourages us to become complete, lacking nothing, as our faith is tested and as our faith becomes evident in works.

For some time, we saw the peace sign. The conscience of this nation has been quickened concerning the issues of war, poverty, and prejudice. We cannot rest until our society finds a more responsible solution to these pressing issues. And *shalom,* peace, became the symbol of a most urgent concern and hope. But this symbol was raised by many involved in some of the most unpeaceful episodes ever witnessed in this land.

Then we began to see the ONE WAY sign which means there is only one way to the abundant life, only one way to solve the problems of man, and this is through faith in Jesus Christ. But we have seen those who raise this sign, running about on a spiritual high, oblivious to those whom Jesus called "the least of these" (Matthew 25:40), who are crying out from the hurt of hunger, sickness, and prejudice. We tend to limit the alternatives and in so doing we lose the wholeness of Christ's Gospel.

I want to argue that there is a third way, a way that preserves the dynamic conviction of the one-wayers and the depth of compassion that has caused others to be concerned for peace. When such compassion and conviction are held in the vital balance of the third way, we will discover the power of Christ's Gospel as it was so evident in Him and in His commandment to love God and love your neighbor as yourself.

The concept of the third way was first suggested to me during a conversation with Elton Trueblood. As renewal has come to Covenant Church, the brilliant thought and forceful writing of this outstanding spokesman of the Christian faith has been a constant source of guidance and inspiration. He argues in his book *Confronting Christ* that responsible Christianity includes two poles, the love of God and concern for others. To cultivate the inner spiritual life and ignore the needs of others is a heresy. Yet love for others which is not based on the love of God will degenerate into superficial secularism. Both of these priorities must be held together in the wholeness and balance of the Christian life. Without one eventually the other will be lost.

At the moment, we have evidence that the movement is away from viable social compassion and that sect groups and holiness groups which would carry things to oppressive extremes and distortions are gaining the center of the scene. An upsurge of interest in evangelism is sweeping the country. Though I am personally very excited about it, many evangelical Christians with social concern are profoundly concerned that once again the balance is escaping us. Two attitudes, both of which are essential, have been harmed by mutual isolation. There are various aspects of the Gospel but any one of these can be stressed in isolation, until it finally becomes almost as much an evil as a good.

The most urgent concern before us for the well-being of our personal lives and the life of the Church is, how can we attain the vital balance which is offered to us by Christ in His Gospel? The wholeness of the Christian life summarized by conviction and compassion can be realized through the concept of relational Christianity.

An exciting style of Christian living is building through interpersonal relationships. We are discovering that the relationships of life, whether with God, with our family, between different races, or between people with differing opinions, do not have to be the context for conflict and alienation, but can be the occasion for healing and growth, joy and expectation.

1. The first step is to *get committed.* Have you come to terms with the claims of Christ upon your life? Be reconciled to God and to one another. The first step is to seek a living personal relationship with Christ. Have I surrendered my life to the Lordship of Jesus Christ without reservation? The strategic step is to surrender self, to ask Christ to take over at the center of life. Okay, you pious preacher, have you done that? No, I haven't. I give him parts of my life and then I will take one of these back and try to run it myself. One thing is certain, the areas of my life which are under His management are in much better shape than the ones I am still trying to manage. Samuel M. Shoemaker, in his book *How to Become a Christian,* offers the

crucial imperative, "We surrender as much of ourselves as we can to as much of Christ as we understand."

2. The second step is to *get honest* with ourselves. Jesus said we are to love our neighbor as ourselves (*see* Mark 12:31). He intends that we have a proper love for ourselves. Countless persons go through life with a low estimate of themselves. We are of infinite value to God, for He has poured out His love for us in the person of Jesus Christ. Many of us are at war with ourselves, harboring attitudes, doubts, and fears which continually pull us down. Once we enter into a relationship with Christ through faith, we can have a new relationship to ourselves. The Bible says: Confess your sins and you shall be forgiven (*see* 1 John 1:9). Discover this secret of a cleansed life and walk in newness of life. Know the worth and potential of your life and that the power of God working through you is unlimited.

3. Third, *get together.* God intends that the relationships with immediate others in your lives be healed. If you have difficulty respecting yourself or knowing the vital power of God at work in your life, it may well be that a jealousy, hatred, or resentment toward another person has been allowed to fester, pouring poison into your life and preventing the flow of God's Spirit into your experience.

Develop the art of affirming the worth of every person with whom you associate. Jesus affirms the worth of every one of us, for He gives Himself to us as we are. This is the heart of the Christian faith. The condition of our lives is not the condition for being accepted. Reach out to another person and affirm some quality in his life you are alert enough to detect.

Then develop the art of being vulnerable to those about you. Lead with your humanity. We are not called to some superpiety or spiritual superiority. Jesus was vulnerable to the hostility and ridicule of those about him. He was acquainted with the fears, doubts, and pains that we know. He relied upon others, asking the disciples to watch and pray with Him.

We have a tendency to hide our inadequacies and hurts from one another. This produces a brittle tension which creates an uneasiness about ourselves and impairs our relationships with others. When we plaster over and cover that crack with various forms of rationalization, things continue to happen to us inwardly which are not healthy and then suddenly that unresolved tension surfaces in some sort of outburst. If you wish to grow in personal faith find one person who is stronger in faith than you are and allow the strength of his faith to lift you. Find one person who wishes to grow in the Christian faith whom you can affirm and with whom you can be vulnerable, confessing mutual needs, seeking in the name of Christ to have those needs met. Ask God to lead others of His choice to you that you may be mutually sustained in the Christian life. Then find one person whose need is greater than yours and let the strength of your faith lift him.

4. Fourth, *get others.* Introduce someone else to personal faith in Christ. Confess your needs and pray for each other. Bring another person into the Christian fellowship you share so it will be evident what God is doing in the lives of people. Make it clear how a person enters the Christian life. In recent months I have had the privilege of training 150 young people and adults to share their faith clearly and sensitively according to God's guidance. Wherever they go each day these people are able to share the hope that is within them. New life and interest is continually awakened around them.

5. Fifth, *get going* in avenues of service. Find the person or problem where there is suffering and distress and give yourself to it. Surprise yourself with a streak of generosity. An official said recently that the problems in our prisons are going to remain until every person on the inside of our prisons has someone on the outside personally concerned for him. The pattern is relational in every case. Our Lord introduced us to this method. This is documented by the New Testament and is being verified in our experience every day.

8

Count It All Joy!

Count it all joy, my brethren, when you meet various trials, for you know that the testing of your faith produces steadfastness. And let steadfastness have its full effect, that you may be perfect and complete, lacking in nothing.

James 1:2-4

"Look, I don't want a lot of pious, high-sounding words and advice. I want something that works. My mind is in a whirl. It is a bad scene. My friends are in trouble. They are all messed up. It is a hassle at home. I haven't the foggiest idea why I'm here or what it is all about. I just want to find something I can count on that will make sense. I want to know if there is anything that can pull it all together for me."

This urgent plea came recently from a teen-ager for whom life was in complete jeopardy, for whom there seemed to be no way out of many intense problems. We began a search to discover a practical approach to decide what one thing was most needed and for which we would trust God by faith. It was difficult to narrow it all down and become specific by identifying her most urgent concern. But this was accomplished and then faith was put to work. Not just faith, sit in the corner and stare at the ceiling, but faith in terms of attitude, expectation, and endeavor. Instead of being problem-obsessed, we became possibility-possessed. Things began to happen and the life of this young lady became overflowing with surprises. She simply put certain practical principles of faith to work. A working faith—this is what James was talking about and what we will be discussing together.

"Count it all joy, my brethren, when you meet various trials. . . ."
James, what in the world are you talking about? You mean I am
supposed to find some sort of joy in every hardship, affliction, and
difficulty that comes to me? Friend, you've got it. That's the faith
principle to be put to work and when you put it to work it's going
to cleanse and strengthen your faith and it's going to produce a quality
of steadfastness within your life that will be produced in no other way.
James, you've got to be kidding. Things are terrible! Business is down,
a friend is in trouble, and my wife is about to leave me. Things are
just bad all the way around and you say, "Count it all for joy." No
way! James, you just don't know how tough life can be. You just
haven't had much experience with the way things are.

James begins his letter by identifying himself as "a servant [slave]
of God and the Lord Jesus Christ" (James 1:1). Slave is the literal
meaning. None of us like the notion of being a slave and people of
the ancient world abhorred it, especially those who were slaves. James
is saying that in thought, attitude, and action he belongs to the Lord.

James writes to the "twelve dispersed tribes" (*see* verse 1). This
refers throughout the Old Testament to the nation of Israel. Since the
ninth century B.C. that nation had been dispersed by famine, war,
pestilence, and oppression all over the face of the earth. They had
some notion of how rough life can be.

But now James is writing to the new Israel, those called together
by the person of Jesus Christ to become the slaves of God in mind,
attitude, and spirit, to be under His direction. This is a litle band of
people who face uncertainty and the severest affliction to which people
have ever been subjected. James, who is the leader of this scattered
little group, says, "Count it all joy, my brethren!" He knows what
hardship is. His soul and his life have been tested and strengthened,
tempered like steel by these trials because through them the power
of God has been able to flow into his life.

How can I grasp some of that power in my life? James makes it
clear that this is possible.

1. First, he says you cannot always do a lot about the things that
happen to you, but *you can do a lot about your attitude toward the*

things that happen. Your attitude can make a tremendous difference in a difficult situation. Character can surpass circumstances!

James, in a translation according to J. B. Phillips, says that the working of faith is going to produce a healthy independence. Now, this is not the independence of building a cozy little corner for myself in this world where I can be comfortable and forget all the affliction and injustice that impinges upon most of the people in the world today. This is to be independent of the circumstances that flow across life, to be free in temperament and outlook rather than bound to the tide of events, to have a steadfastness and a deliberateness which cannot be carried to and fro by every wind that blows.

The ship of life has a rudder, is headed toward a destination, and we are neither upset nor thrown off course by all the storms that pound us. James speaks of this as maturity of character and the chief quality of such character is steadfastness, endurance. Endurance *(hupomonē)* is not simply to bear things in stoic solemnity but aggressively to meet difficulty and to vanquish it, to turn trouble into triumph. This is a magnificent quality, but how do we possess it? First, James says attitude and outlook are crucial.

2. Second, James says simply and practically, *welcome the trial,* greet the difficulty, embrace the horror of defeat, pain, tragedy, disappointment, or dreaded happening. That's pretty heavy! J. B. Phillips translates James 1:1,2: "When all kinds of trials and temptations crowd into your lives, my brothers, don't resent them as intruders, but welcome them as friends!" Listen, I even resent getting a cold. I get mad at the world when I can't find my keys or date book in the morning and this can make all of life tenuous for ensuing hours. Life gets messed up and I resent anyone whom I can implicate. Count it all joy! When you meet every kind of trial, recognize that it comes to cleanse and strengthen your faith and produce the quality of steadfastness.

When I spoke these words from Covenant's pulpit some months ago a member in good standing sat there shaking her head. "That just could never work for me." Suddenly she had an experience which opened a totally new dimension to her life. Without warning her mother died. There were issues between herself and her mother that had never been resolved and this young woman was seized with an overwhelming sense of guilt. Her mother was a wonderful woman of profound and godly faith, but there were a few things they both would do differently if they had the opportunity to do them all over again. She tried everything possible on her own to resolve this agony that was tearing her to pieces, but she could not face it.

Finally Alice called a friend who was not overly pious but close to life, and she asked the friend to pray for her. Alice says this was the most difficult thing she has ever had to do in her life. She felt self-sufficient and the spiritual dimension of life was not a dominant interest to her. She was a superactivist. Now she was asking a friend to pray for her.

She went home for the funeral, at first abhorring every part of the journey. But then a strange peace that even amazed her husband began to fall over her. The words from James came to her, from where she did not know, but suddenly that was all that was in her mind. "Count it all joy when you meet all kinds of trials, don't resent them as intruders, but welcome them as friends."

"Suddenly I sensed that what was happening to me was that I was recovering the wondrous faith and love of my mother which we had never quite shared completely. I had the profound sense that all was well because her prayers for me were being accomplished, that she was at home with God and one day we would be reunited.

"I had dreaded the funeral, but throughout the time of meeting countless people the richest, fondest, most beautiful expressions of love were flowing everywhere which I probably would never have noticed if my heart had not been opened to let Christ come into my life. So much has been given to me, I just have to give it to others. The whole world looks different."

This woman had been a total activist, she held profound compassion for all who are victims of society. She continues to hold that compassion to which Christ calls us, but now she holds a deep commitment to Christ Himself. She has found and is living mightily in the strength, balance, and wholeness of the third way.

I am not an outstanding example of this principle of welcoming, engaging, and living victoriously with every situation, but I cherish it and pray that it is becoming inherent in my life, for I have had it lived out magnificently about me all my life, and it is the richest possession that could ever come to a man or woman. For as long as I can remember, my mother, who is gentle and humble, has encouraged me to greet the worst experience and welcome the person who troubles me most. To dread, fear, run, abhor, is to be overtaken and defeated. Count it all joy, for when such testing is so received it produces strength to bear still more and to conquer in still more difficult battles. Recently, death and intense suffering impinged upon my mother and she lived radiantly and joyfully amidst it all. What a working faith! We recognize that our attitudes are important; the quality of our attitude is built by welcoming trials in the confidence of what God can accomplish through them in our lives.

3. Third, James exhorts us, "Let steadfastness [which is being built within you] have its full effect, that you may be perfect and complete, lacking in nothing." Jesus said, "Blessed are you when men revile you and persecute you and utter all kinds of evil against you falsely on my account. Rejoice and be glad . . ." (Matthew 5:11). Read that by itself and it sounds like nonsense. But here is this principle at the conclusion of the Beatitudes, the summary of Jesus' entire imperative to us. It is the same principle found in the first few verses of James. Then we hear Paul in the fifth chapter of Romans saying:

> . . . we rejoice in our sufferings, knowing that suffering produces endurance, and endurance produces character, and character produces hope, and hope does not disappoint us, because God's love has been poured into our hearts through the Holy Spirit which has been given to us.
>
> Romans 5:3-5

Here is this faith principle of *steadfastness* that is being built up within us as we are able to receive the difficulties and the shattering

67

disappointments counting it for joy, trusting God to work His perfect purpose through it all.

James is still pressing us, however. He says you have begun to realize this quality of steadfastness and what God can do through such staying power. This new depth of character begins to become a reality in our lives. James says let steadfastness follow through to its full consequence so you become more and more complete as a person.

He doesn't let up for a second. You and I know in almost any area of life we can fail to follow through. There are many sports we enjoy. But we know how serious it is not to follow through when we are throwing or swinging. It can upset our balance and effectiveness. We may be just getting our golf swing grooved, but then there is no follow-through and the ball just will not go straight and true to the final objective. The golf swing is effective when it flows through to its full consequence.

Once we begin to realize what the Christian life is all about we tend to think we have it made, but this is the strategic moment when we must allow it to flow forth clear through to its total consequence. God will continue His work within you so that you may become the whole person in thinking, feeling, and doing that you were created to be.

9

Faith Completed by Love

Be doers of the word, and not hearers only. . . .
Religion that is pure and undefiled before God and the Father is
this: to visit orphans and widows in their affliction. . . . What does
it profit, my brethren, if a man says he has faith but has not works?
Can his faith save him? . . . So faith by itself, if it has no works,
is dead. . . .
By my works [I] will show you my faith.

James 1:22,27; 2:14,17,18

If we take seriously the imperative of Christ we realize that the
words above are the consequence of His compassion for us, the compassion He hopes we will have for one another. These verses express
the very epitome of personal faith as applied to social concern. Every
aspect of the teachings of Jesus encourages us to invest portions of
our time and resources, our very lives in the interests and welfare of
other human beings. This is religion pure and undefiled before God.
This is faith completed through love. James emphasized the role of
the will in the Christian life as faith becomes evident in action. Faith
is completed by what we do and faith is seriously incomplete when
it fails to make a difference in the way we live.

The Bible leaves the demand for social justice upon us: "What doth
the Lord require of thee, but to do justly, and to love mercy, and to
walk humbly with thy God?" (Micah 6:8 KJV). Jesus left us with the
clear imperative that to ignore the needy is to reject our Lord Himself,
and to stand under God's judgment. To receive the person who is
hungry, thirsty, sick, or imprisoned is to receive Christ, and to abandon these persons who are in need is to abandon Christ and to risk
separation from Him (*see* Matthew 25:31-46).

James says you can know the Word of God completely but if you do not live according to that Word it is all in vain. Authentic religion, a living relationship with God, is evident when we do such things as visit orphans and widows in their difficulties (*see* James1:27). If you try to ignore the physical suffering in your own community where the odds are against an underprivileged child finishing high school, against his gaining training essential to break out of the poverty, delinquency, and deprived cycle, you are at enmity with God and your neighbor. If you are unmoved by the fact that two-thirds of the children in the world go to sleep hungry and that more than one-third of the world's people live with sickness that leaves them drained, ineffective, and listless, then you live in darkness and the light is not in you (*see* 1 John 2:11). "This is his commandment, that we should believe in the name of his Son Jesus Christ and love one another . . ." (1 John 3:23).

You may have made a bold profession of faith in Christ and you may have an impressive testimony of what God has done in your life, but if you have not moved out personally and deliberately to alleviate the physical suffering of others, your faith is incomplete, and James questions whether such faith is real or capable of saving you (*see* James 2:14). Jesus says your life is like a tree that has not borne the fruit for which it was intended and is good for nothing but to be cut down and cast into the fire (*see* Matthew 3:10).

To trust in Christ means to rely upon Him alone and to rely upon Him alone means to take Him at His Word. His Word is, "Love your neighbor as yourself" (Mark 12:31). And according to His Word our neighbor is anyone in need regardless of his condition or how he came to be in that condition. Our love for others is evidence that we have fellowship with God and know the wonder of His love for all of us. God's love is unconditional, spontaneous, and offered to all people.

If a person is ill-clad and hungry and all you do is pray for him, James says you are a spiritual prude. If you simply say, "I sure hope you keep warm and find food," but you do nothing to supply his bodily needs, what is the good of that? This is empty faith without corresponding life and work. It is useless and dead, for it does not lead to action (*see* James 2:17). It is of no practical good to your neighbor and you raise a question about the reality of your own salvation: ". . . if a man says he has faith but has not works? Can his faith save him?" (James 2:14). James says, "I will not talk about my faith until you can see it in my actions." He says, "Our faith is made complete by what we do."

The faith of Abraham, the Old Testament patriarch, was an active faith. He was willing to fulfill God's entire commandment, though this was dreadfully demanding. To fulfill the commandment of love is difficult, but this is the law to which we are held accountable:

> We know that we have passed out of death into life, because we love the brethren. He who does not love remains in death. . . . But if any one has the world's goods and sees his brother in need, yet closes his heart against him, how does God's love abide in him?
>
> 1 John 3:14,17

Then there was Rahab, the harlot. That word *harlot* bothers us, doesn't it? James tells us that this filthy woman was probably closer to God than some of us with all our spiritual sophistication, for the simple reason that she was humble enough to receive those who were in trouble and to help them (*see* James 2:25). Startling, isn't it? Just as the body without the spirit of life is dead, so faith without works is empty and futile (*see* James 2:26).

It is startling to remember that the educational, cultural, and economic opportunities most of us enjoy put us among the most richly endowed people in all history. We are among the richest 5 percent of the world's population. The average income in the rest of the world is two hundred dollars a year. We are going to have to decide why we are among the most gifted people ever to have inhabited the earth. Our standard of living, the pleasures we enjoy, our vocational training make us rich and enable us to partake of fruits beyond anything ever experienced by the vast majority of humanity on this earth.

If you advance from one pleasure to another as your income increases, if you suppose all of this is your own to enjoy and to do with as you please, James says your commitment to Christ lacks an essential dimension and God holds you accountable (*see* James 5:1). Everything you possess is given to you in trust from God. Jesus tells us in a parable that a servant faithfully held what the master had entrusted to him. But that servant was under condemnation simply because he did not increase the talents entrusted to him by the lord to be put into service (*see* Matthew 25).

If you, who are among the richest people in all of history, use your material resources only for your own comfort, pleasure, and security, then you are content to grind the faces of the poor in the dust and you better remember that their cries reach the ears of the Lord of hosts (*see* James 5:4). James says you are actually guilty of fraud because you have misused what was entrusted to you to use and invest in such a way that those who are disadvantaged might find opportunity to break out of the cycle of illiteracy, hunger, and sickness.

Let us not rationalize. "I deserve what I have and enjoy. I worked for it and it is mine." Did you deserve to be born? Did you deserve to be born free? Did you deserve to be born without mental and physical handicaps? Did you deserve to be born to your parents or into the midst of unlimited opportunity?

When men like ourselves honestly consider the privileges we enjoy, when we consider a world bound to subsistence and below subsistence levels, when our conscience is awakened by the mind of Christ, we have no alternative but to confess humbly that all we have and are is of God, entrusted to us to be used in the service of humanity, and that Christ has a claim upon our every decision concerning the use of these resources, especially when we consider luxury, pleasure, and comfort.

When we consider how the black man in our society is locked into a cycle of poverty, despair, and overpopulation, when we consider the similar pattern that engulfs the uneducated white where only an isolated person can put together the ingredients to escape to something better, and when we consider the dehumanizing condition of the congested city ghetto and the pollution of man's environment, we can only conclude that the resources entrusted to us are the means for lifting the condition of human life and are not ours to do with as we please. Paul said that it is out of our abundance that God intends that their needs shall be supplied (*see* 2 Corinthians 9:6-15).

Some months ago a member of Covenant's Fellowship of Christian Sharing was calling on needy families in our county. A school nurse had asked us to investigate what seemed to be a serious problem. We have found that welfare and other public agencies are often unable to solve the problems of those who are bound to poverty, sickness, and despair. This Sharing Fellowship has been the only means in the county through which food, medical attention, and guidance have been available to many who are in need. The public agencies have come to rely heavily upon the trained Christian Sharing workers.

Our caller came to a tar-paper shack surrounded by abandoned cars. A small, ill-clad child opened the door and stood in the bitter winter cold. There was no heat inside so the small children were almost frozen. The mother and a school-age child lay sick and helpless. The father had abandoned his family ten days before. Medical attention, heat, food, and clothing were provided. Several calls a day were necessary to clean, attend, and encourage.

Finally everyone was ready to go out. Though we supply vast amounts of good used clothing, we attempt to go with each person we are helping so he can buy new underwear and shoes. When these children came out of the store wearing their new shoes they seemed to stand ten feet tall. Conscious concern identified particular needs and met them in a way that was uplifting to the individuals. When the question was asked, "Why did you do this for us?" the only answer that was given was, "We want to do this because Christ loves all of us."

Some weeks later the father returned. Several of our men began to work with him. Though it has been a difficult, slow process, he is now working regularly and caring for a healthy family.

10
Let's Be Practical!

Happy is the man who remains faithful under trials; for when he
succeeds in passing the test he will be given life, the prize which
God has promised to those who love him.

James 1:12 TEV

Our first question about anything today is, "Will it work?" We want
to know if it will make money or get votes. Will it enable us to solve
a problem or to do something better? When a new dictating machine
is made, the primary imperative is, "Make it work!" It is not surprising that these same pragmatic values become applied to people. The
man who can "get the job done" is worth one hundred thousand. If
he fails to produce for six months, his worth is gone and so is he.
When something fails to work, it is no longer of any value.

William James, Charles Peirce, and John Dewey formulated philo-
sophical pragmatism. Dewey said that truth is not a copy of tran-
scendent or absolute truth. An idea can be said to "work" only when
actions based on it lead to predictable results. Every truth has practical consequences, and these are the test of its truth, according to
Peirce.

Our education materials and our everyday way of thinking are filled
with the concepts of pragmatism. It is fair to ask the pragmatic
question, "What are the consequences of pragmatism?" One of the
primary consequences is that we live in what Cornelius A. Van
Peursen, in "Man and Reality—The History of Human Thought,"
calls a "functional era." We have passed from the mystical and from
the ontological to the functional stage. In this functional stage,
whether or not the fathers of pragmatism intended it, our model has

become the machine. So we find that people are being treated impersonally. We are being computerized and given numbers rather than names with individual identities. The youth of our day have recognized the tragic consequences of expecting people to function like machines. Youth cry out, "Quit destroying me! I'm a person, not a machine."

William Glasser, in his book *Identity Society,* argues that our civilization is going through a major transformation which is from a goal-oriented to a role-oriented society. Last spring I married a couple the day after they graduated from Purdue University. Forty-eight hours later their friends had dispersed forever. These friends had been the audience before whom they played a role. They didn't question the role; they were simply concerned with playing their role with "class." Without an audience they had no role, and without a role they were lost. There was no goal providing an integrating, motivating force in their lives.

There are dire consequences to secular pragmatism, for the question of purpose is not adequately answered. How does a society set its purpose? Do we leave this to an intellectual elite, to a select group such as controls Soviet Russia, or do we accept whatever 51 percent of the people support, which would have made the acts of Hitler justified. How do we determine the purposes for which an idea can be judged workable or unworkable? Without an awareness of absolutes society is without a sustaining purpose and people play roles which are senseless. There is a personal quality to human life and the purpose of the personal is unexplainable apart from the Person who set the values by which the personal is meaningfully preserved in human experience.

James was writing to a people who were struggling to preserve values which they had come to believe to be absolutely essential to life. Their personal lives had meaning and purpose because of a personal God who had spoken quite clearly concerning the only basis upon which men can ultimately live. A few people do not determine this; 51 percent of the people do not determine it; God has so created us.

James raised practical issues. He called for personal honesty, aware that sham, superficial pride, and arrogance are devisive: "Have you not made distinctions among yourselves, and become judges with evil thoughts?" (James 2:4). He also knew that if men put their allegiance in the things or standards of the world, they will never know God or that which is essential to their lives: "Do you not know that friendship with the world is enmity with God?" (4:4).

James addressed "the twelve tribes in the Dispersion," by which he meant any Christian anywhere who might face a number of formidable challenges to his faith. So the concerns of James were primarily practical. He was concerned about what would finally work as an adequate basis for human life. He was concerned with discovering a working faith which would enable us to become complete persons lacking nothing which is essential to our well-being. Men have realized that the biblical faith offers the only practical answer to the problems of life. Nothing else will ultimately work. The aim James had was to help people discover how they can have completeness of character.

James said it was a very practical matter:

> Happy is the man who remains faithful under trials; for when he succeeds in passing the test he will be given life, the prize which God has promised to those who love him.

> James 1:12 TEV

James knew that every Christian faces severe testing in the form of hardship, disappointment, and suffering. These trials *(peirasmos)* are first, enemies which confront us from without causing serious difficulty *(see* 1:2-4). Second, these trials come from within and are in the form of temptations which provide a formidable threat to our well-being *(see* 1:13,14). The inward testing comes in the form of our own evil desires. The trials James was concerned about are not primarily persecution as in First Peter 1:6; 2:9. The trials faced by the people to whom James wrote were hardships from without and temptations from within. The chief threat James saw was that these trials from without and within would undermine the Christian's steadfastness or determination to remain faithful when tested. The Greek word is *hupomonē* and, as we have seen in chapter 8, refers to the steadfast determination to triumph. This endurance arises from a steadfast trust that God will work His good purpose through us no matter how devastating our trials become. The person "who remains faithful under trials" will be the truly happy man because he will discover the full promise of God for him.

Faith *(pistis)*, according to James, is the attitude of a person's whole being through which he comes to share in the complete purpose of God for His people (*see* 1:6; 2:1,5,14). James Hardy Ropes, in the *International Critical Commentary, Epistle of St. James,* says that James saw trials as either building the strength of faith as a complete and forceful quality of life or as imperiling the persistence of faith and thus separating us from the source and center of life, which is God. Steadfastness *(hupomonē)* of faith leads from strength to strength for it is founded upon God and not the changing conditions surrounding our lives.

Steadfastness refers to a quality of life, a constant and dependable characteristic of a personality by which all actions are influenced. This quality of life is a gift of God which grows in depth when we put it to work. "Thou, O Lord, art my hope, my trust . . ." (Psalms 71:5). "Then they left the presence of the council, rejoicing that they were counted worthy to suffer dishonor for the name" (Acts 5:41; *see* also Romans 10:11; Matthew 5:11). James encourages us to build, develop, and exercise this quality of steadfastness—it works! This is a completely practical matter.

The steadfast person is truly happy because his life is properly founded. "He will receive as his reward the life which God has promised him" (*see* James 1:12). Literally James says, "He will receive the crown of life." A crown was worn at wedding feasts and other occasions of joy. Steadfastness and joy are inseparable. Through steadfastness, strength of character is built. As we face the demands of life more and more effectively we have the joy of knowing how God seeks to complete our lives according to the fullness of His purpose for us. Here is a faith that works when applied to the practical problems of each day. This faith is life-building.

Florence is a capable, radiant, mature, loving person. It was not surprising that she was elected a deacon and was completely able to take this responsibility and to care for her wonderful family. Soon she was working with children in the blighted area of Lafayette in a neighborhood-development program sponsored by our deacons' board. She effectively taught handicraft to a class of children. The lives of these children were lifted by her love for them. However, she was continually discouraged by the fact that although the children did well so long as she was with them, when they left her they fell into all sorts of difficulty. There was no "staying force" in their lives.

Betty was the mother of one of these childern and was a derelict alcoholic. She was the vicitm of every unhealthy practice and was destroying the life of her daughter. With strong determination, Florence set out to help Betty get a job and clean up her life. Her love enabled Betty to land several jobs but she always fell back.

During one short period between Florence's visits, a small group of people began to meet with Betty and introduced her to the power of prayer and personal faith in Christ. The next time Florence visited, she immediately realized that Betty was a new person. For the first time she was clean, attractively dressed, alert, and had a regular job. She had allowed God to build and strengthen her personal faith.

Florence realized that she had never allowed herself, her family, or the children she was trying to help to discover the full force of personal faith in God which is the one quality of life capable of sustaining a person no matter what circumstances and stress befall him. She opened her life, asking God to build such a steadfast faith in her as the staying power to the love she had for others. She has discovered that love for others is made complete through steadfast trust in God. It works! Ask Florence and Betty. They know and are sharing with others the completeness of personal faith and active love.

11

Becoming a More Complete Person
Through Prayer

And let steadfastness have its full effect, that you may be perfect
and complete, lacking in nothing. If any of you lacks wisdom, let
him ask God, who gives to all men generously and without re-
proaching, and it will be given him. But let him ask in faith, with
no doubting, for he who doubts is like a wave of the sea that is driven
and tossed by the wind.

James 1:4-6

A young couple had come to Purdue, where he was to finish a Ph.D.
degree in industrial management. He left a high-paying job in business
searching for personal fulfillment which continually eluded him. Bill
and Sue had no clear-cut sense of personal identity or understanding
of their relationship to each other. They threw themselves into the
exciting activities of this academic community which left them exhausted rather than fulfilled. They were "driven and tossed" by many
influences until they doubted themselves and each other.

They were invited to a prayer-and-Bible-study group, which was
the most boring and ridiculous idea they could imagine. They went
only because they wanted to win the favor of a neighbor who invited
them. They were uncomfortable through the whole meeting and when
invited back they returned only to win favor with the group. After
some time, Bill recognized a deliberate and dynamic quality in the
lives of the men. Sue began to find direction coming into her life. They
came closer to each other as they began to discover what was lacking
in their lives. These "double-minded" people who had been unstable

in their ways, "driven and tossed" by conflicting influences, found their lives becoming more and more complete.

James speaks of letting "steadfastness" of faith have its "full effect" that we may become "complete." The Greek word for "complete" is *hŏlŏklērŏs* and describes the personal wholeness coming bit by bit as weaknesses and imperfections are removed from our personalities through a consistent trust in Christ. This growth continues as what is lacking is graciously supplied. The imagery James uses is of an army determined to reach its objective, refusing to give up in the struggle. The person who meets his testing with steadfast trust in what God will accomplish through every event will move from victory to victory rather than from defeat to defeat.

How do we become more complete as a person? James gives us two principles for discovering the victory of a fulfilled life: (1) Become specific in prayer and (2) Become deliberate in action.

1. *Become specific in prayer.* James says if you do not know how to meet a problem ask God, who gives generously, and all your needs will be met (*see* James 1:5). I began to experience God's power for resolving the distressing dilemmas of my life when I became specific in prayer, identifying what I need most and deliberately trusting God to provide for that need.

The effectiveness of specific prayer became even more powerful when I dared to become public in those requests which were made of God. To offer specific prayer in the presence of others is an act which develops the capacity to trust God by faith, believing and doubting not. This practice builds the strength to take the risk that what is prayed for may be refused. We leave the dreary and depressing confines of worry and weakness, moving out where we are no longer bound by old limitations, where we have the opportunity of discovering new possibilities.

Prayer becomes effective when we dare to identify our most critical need and when we dare to pray openly with fellow Christians, trusting God to meet that need. Our lives will become complete; what is lacking will be provided when we pray specifically in the presence of others for what may be refused, trusting God to provide all that is necessary. When I have practiced this principle I have found an answer and a provision opened to me which I would never have seen if I had forced my own plans and pressed for results from my own efforts:

> Have no anxiety about anything, but in everything by prayer and supplication with thanksgiving let your requests be made known to God. And the peace of God, which passes all understanding, will keep your hearts and your minds in Christ Jesus.
>
> Philippians 4:6,7

First, we become more complete persons when we become specific in prayer.

2. *Become deliberate in action.* James offers the clear imperative, "Be doers of the word and not hearers only . . ." (James 1:22). "What does it profit, my brethren, if a man says he has faith but has not works? Can his faith save him?" (2:14). "Faith by itself, if it has no works, is dead . . . . I by my works will show you my faith" (2:17,18). James is articulating the biblical principle that the reality of our faith is seen in our actions. Jesus said, "You will know them by their fruits . . ." (Matthew 7:16) . Paul spoke of being "filled with the fruits of righteousness which come through Jesus Christ" (Philippians 1:11). Works and fruits are a demonstration that we have been restored to a right relationship with God (justified) through faith in Christ.

Effective action is in line with what we most fully believe and know about God and is not impetuous or aimless. When we act our trust is not in our own efforts but in what God can accomplish through efforts which are open to His direction. Frequently we act by faith, having no idea what the outcome will be. Our actions are never blind but always directed by God's Word, reason, and Christian experience. On many occasions it is more Christian to act than pray. Life is made complete when prayer and action are inseparably related.

Frank Laubach has written the Christian classic, *Prayer, the Might-*

iest Force in the World. While lecturing a few years ago, Dr. Laubach told how he had been asked if this title of his famous book still expressed his convictions. He said,"I would express it this way now: Prayer is the mightiest force in the world when a person is willing to do something besides pray." Frank Laubach is an outstanding example of one who has put faith into practice, who has kept prayer and action in their dynamic and proper relationship, who has been specific in prayer and deliberate in action. He has taught thousands to pray and he has taught thousands to read. Such a balanced, healthy life of prayer and endeavor supplies what is lacking, making life complete. He has carried his literacy plan of "each one teach one" into the most deprived areas of the world. He has done this prayerfully and practically.

Two years ago my mother sank to the lowest depths of physical strength. All that was left was the will to believe and the will to live. Then even that began to waver for both Mother and Dad. Would my faith weaken when I entered that hospital room and saw her suffering and uncertainty?

Before I left for Crystal Lake, Illinois, I met with that small group of Christians through whom a few years before I had been privileged to discover how complete and unlimited the power of God is. Because of their faith, I prayed without doubting in their midst and immediately drove for three hours to my mother's side. As I entered that room, I knew I was accompanied by the power of the Holy Spirit. I prayed publicly and specifically that night that she would be healed and that she would be able to come to Lafayette and join in prayer and praise with those who sustained her in prayer. Strength rallied and confidence grew.

When I had returned home the doctor stunned my parents with the news that in her weakened condition Mother had contracted another disease. Immediately every fear Mother and Dad had ever known fell full weight upon them. Discouragement of a weakened condition took over. I was seized with sorrow when I heard of the new suffering my mother had to bear. But Vivian and the group of

Christians with whom I openly confessed my sorrow would not let me give in to doubt.

As my parents and I were once again together on a dark night of uncertainty, the Spirit of Christ began to dwell in us, to take over in our thoughts, feelings, and will. We began to become complete in faith and outlook and Mother began to be healed.

At about half-past four the next morning, Mother awakened with the desperate sense that she was dying. There was no way she could call or signal for help. She was utterly and horribly alone. She heard vividly the words "Esther Tozer is nothing, nothing, nothing!" She felt that as a person she was completely dead. Then she heard, "I have been crucified with Christ; it is no longer I who live, but Christ who lives in me; and the life I now live in the flesh I live by faith in the Son of God, who loved me and gave himself for me" (Galatians 2:20).

From that moment she experienced new life, strength, and health. It was a long road to recovery but she had the faith which worked mightily through prayer to make her complete, lacking nothing. We had asked in faith not doubting at all. It was the faith of those about us which sustained our faith! A year later sixty people who had never been in a group for prayer, sharing, and Bible study met for the first time in our living room to start a new group. I had hoped for twelve people and God sent sixty. That evening my mother was present to share for the first time her joy for the new life God had given her through severe trial and suffering.

Life becomes complete when first, we are specific in prayer and second, when we are deliberate in action. This life of prayer and effort is sustained by the confidence of what God can do on all occasions and by the willingness to respond with our lives the best we can. Rather than being driven and tossed by conflicting influences, we have the stabiltiy of a life which is oriented in God through the prayer of faith and the life of responsible endeavor.

12

The Fellowship of Healing

Is any one among you suffering? Let him pray. Is any cheerful? Let him sing praise. Is any among you sick? Let him call the elders of the church, and let them pray over him, anointing him with oil in the name of the Lord; and the prayer of faith will save the sick man, and the Lord will raise him up. . . .

James 5:13-15

Sickness enters the experience of each one of us. Sickness may be the dreadful curtailment of life, or it may be the occasion for discovering the unlimited power and peace of God's presence. Medical science is making fabulous advances in overcoming disease. As a pastor, I have faced a myriad of diseases with people, and surrounding the memory of these experiences there is a host of nurses, doctors, attendants, workers, and volunteers who are the servants of God, whom He is using through their dedication to heal people medically.

But for all the healing that takes place, there are countless persons whose lives are filled with pain from sickness which could be healed by the power of God. God intends that our lives be whole and healthy. There is intense anguish and pain which could be replaced by assurance and health. Matthew records that Jesus healed Peter's mother-in-law and the Gospel writer concludes, "This was to fulfill what was spoken by the prophet Isaiah, 'He took our infirmities and bore our diseases' " (Matthew 8:17). About 60 percent of Jesus' activities upon earth, as portrayed for us in the Gospels, were to heal the afflictions of people.

Jesus Christ is present among us in the full power of the Holy Spirit and He seeks to heal us spiritually and physically. The intention of

God is that we be made whole and at one with Him. When we talk about healing, it is always a danger that interest in physical healing will overshadow the critical importance of the healing of a person's inner spiritual life. Whenever the gifts of the Spirit are discussed, there is the danger that the gifts rather than the Giver will dominate the discussion. We seek only to hold up before men Jesus Christ and the wholeness of life, physical and spiritual, to which He calls us. When we have been made one with God, we will experience healing within our inner lives. When we come into a living relationship with God through personal trust in Christ, unhealthy attitudes and moods are going to begin to be cleared up and we are going to become more complete persons. When this kind of healing is taking place within our inner lives and a living relationship with God is being established, we have the best possible conditions for the healing of physical diseases.

For some of us sickness is the most pressing concern of life. For others, it is the furthest thought from our minds, but some of us will be suddenly stunned by the fact that we are sick and that the sickness in our life has to be dealt with. What can we do? Before we consider James's suggestion, there are two factors we need to mention.

First: The first reaction to sickness is, "Why me?" Some people move to the next step and surrender themselves to the will of God, asking Him to heal them in the confidence that He can accomplish some good purpose out of this whole experience even though it may not be what they want. When I am sick, I do not suppose my reaction will be particularly great. I do not want spiritual prudes offering advice. I want spiritually mature people with whom to share my fears and doubts; with whom to pray for healing in the confidence that God can heal, that whatever happens His good purpose will be accomplished, and that it can all be counted for joy. I do not want any of these "ifs" or "maybes." I want to pray for healing according to James 5:13,15; Philippians 4:6; Matthew 7:7; "Whatever you ask in my name, I will do it . . ." (John 14:13).

Second: Many of us are spiritually weak because we have not witnessed spiritual strength. We have been conditioned by a blind, earth-bound outlook to rely only upon what we can do or know for ourselves and to shy away from anything which God alone can do or make known to us. When we deliberately place our trust in God, we gain a new perspective discovering the abundant, sound, rational evidence verifying the wisdom and necessity of trusting in what God can accomplish through any event in our lives, no matter how difficult. When we make this commitment, we live in the expectation and confidence of what God can do. He does amazing things. Our faith is built up. Our experience of His power grows. We discover how practical and down-to-earth His power can be.

The conviction is arising at the grass-roots level in the Church that God does not intend that vast numbers of people flounder in sickness and distress simply because they have never heard that vast and unlimited power is available to them. People are discovering that there is power to heal! So, fellowships of prayer and healing are being formed in congregations of every denomination.

James gives us specific guidance for when sickness comes:

"Is any among you sick? Let him call for the elders of the church, and let them pray over him, anointing him with oil in the name of the Lord; and the prayer of faith will save the sick man, and the Lord will raise him up. . . .

James 5:14,15

A few years ago, I discovered personally the deep resources of God's spiritual power through the fellowship of prayer on Wednesday evenings. God's Holy Spirit opened up to me the awesome awareness of how unlimited the power and love of God actually are. I vowed then that I, as pastor, would never stand in the way of a member of my flock discovering the power which can make all things possible, that I would get myself out of the way and let God's power flow directly into human life.

That covenant had no more than been made when a member of the church, a big, tough, well-known businessman who had suffered with physical affliction for eight years, called me. He informed me that he had come to the end, he could not endure another day, his mental attitude was shot, and he was in despair. Ordinarily, I would have given him a pep talk or a book, and tried in my own strength of persuasion to lift his outlook. I had done that for ten years. It is like trying to put your shoulder under a corner of the universe to raise it. If you have a "down day," you let everyone down. I remembered my vow and offered an invitation for him to come to the Wednesday-evening fellowship of prayer. He was so weak and in such pain that it was impossible for him to get into his car. I offered to bring the members of the prayer fellowship to his home. He said, "Do it, I am ready."

We arrived, sang hymns, testified to faith, heard this man's request for prayer and healing. We prayed, and in that moment he sensed the power of God's Holy Spirit entering into the afflicted area of his body, and he was healed. He has openly and joyfully borne witness to what God had done before many people.

Do you know what I was thinking about the whole time these folks were praying? Do you know what I was sitting there doing that whole time? I was worrying, "What will happen if this doesn't work?" Impressive, isn't it? This is a typical freshman attitude toward healing. However, a great God excused my doubt and heard the prayer of faith offered by the laymen. I have not really graduated much beyond that, but the Lord has lifted my vision so that now, when we enter into the fellowship of prayer and healing, I do not try to lift this person with my spirit or worry about being embarrassed if my "thing" does not work. I am hopeful only that this person will come into the stream of God's Spirit and I fully expect God to do something good. And He does every time. I have come to know many persons who could stand and affirm the healing power of God in their lives. A tremendous healing has occurred in the life of a woman recently and her whole family is filled with joy and gratitude.

There is a healing fellowship at work and if a person asks this fellowship to come, they will come and pray with him. The fellowship is made up of strong, responsible men and gracious women in whom the love and power of God are evident. When the need arises, these laymen will drop everything in order to show their concern and offer prayer. When the elders are called, according to James 5:14 they will come and share in the fellowship of prayer and healing. A person may simply ask that we pray for him in our private prayers. I personally pray every morning and night for numerous persons. It is the healthiest thing I do all day. I forget myself for a little while. This is the fellowship of the concerned, a fellowship of healing.

Anointing with oil bothers some people. It especially bothered me when a family asked me to anoint a girl who was sick. They had read Mark 6:13, where the disciples of Jesus "anointed with oil many that were sick and healed them." I had the image of taking a bottle of some kind of messy oil and pouring it all over a sick person's head. I remembered the Twenty-Third Psalm: "Thou anointest my head with oil." I knew that this was a channel of God's healing and compassion. I knew that with the sacrament of God's grace in baptism and Holy Communion, we use a visible substance: bread, wine, and water. But anointing with oil had me wondering.

I asked a close friend who is an outstanding scientist to go with me. We had to travel sixty miles to the hospital. When we walked into the room the girl was in an oxygen tent. She smiled when she saw us, for she had been praying that we would come. Here I was, the great spiritual leader again! But all I was worrying about was that my friend would get oil on everything. I just expected that there would be oil all over the bed and certainly the people in charge of the hospital would not care for us making such a mess. Really, this was all I could think about.

To my relief, my friend knew what he was doing. You see, I did not have the courage to admit that I did not have the vaguest notion of how this was to be done. Here I was, an ordained man who had been to seminary, read Tillich, Niebuhr, and Bultmann, could read James 5:14 in Greek and parse most of the verbs, but it never occurred to me that anyone might actually wish to be anointed with oil anymore. Of course the disciples did it and James commanded it.

My friend took a little flask of oil from his inside pocket, poured a few drops on his fingers, explained what he was doing, reached into the oxygen tent, and placed his fingers on the girl's forehead. I had taken the girl's hand. We were joined in the fellowship of prayer all around that bed. Clearly and unmistakably, as we prayed, we sensed the power of the Holy Spirit filling each of us and that whole room with the prevailing presence of God and lifting every one of our lives until we knew God's power and what He can do. In that experience you are delivered from worry whether or not the person is healed. You have come with the person who is sick into the full presence of God, the fullest possibility for healing has been established, and you are utterly confident of what God will do. Whatever happens, that person is with God.

I had never expected to see that girl walk on the face of this earth again because of the disease that had afflicted her body. God restored strength to this girl and enabled her to rise from her bed.

Let us again hear the Word of God as it is recorded in the fifth chapter of James, verses 13,14, and 15:

> . . . Is any cheerful? Let him sing praise. Is any among you sick? Let him call the elders of the church, and let them pray over him, anointing him with oil in the name of the Lord; and the prayer of faith will save the sick man, and the Lord will raise him up. . . .

III

The Balanced Life—
It Has to Be!—Peter

13

Come Home!

Peter, an apostle of Jesus Christ, To the exiles of the Dispersion in Pontus, Galatia, Cappadocia, Asia, and Bithynia, chosen and destined by God the Father and sanctified by the Spirit for obedience to Jesus Christ and for sprinkling with his blood:

1 Peter 1:1,2

"Come home to Greece!" is the invitation offered on an airlines poster. When you walk to the Acropolis or stand in the Parthenon, in an important sense, you are going home. Your cultural roots, the origins of your civilization and of your very life are rediscovered there and you are at home.

In one of the most dramatic scenes in the movie *Patton,* the forceful general is bouncing along in his starred jeep with his driver on a desolate road in Tunisia, North Africa. It's just after the terrible American defeat at Kasserine Pass. General Dwight D. Eisenhower has personally ordered Patton to take command of the Second Corps and prepare it for combat. Patton has just stunned these men with word of what his discipline means and what trials of combat are before them. Now he is going out alone to see the gruesome sight at Kasserine Pass.

Suddenly he startles his driver: "Turn!" The driver can't see where or why to turn. "Turn!" They lurch down into a gully, climb over a ridge, and there before them is the Carthaginian plain where one of the most splendid cities of ancient time had stood, where for two years the Roman legions of Scipio Africanus besieged the city, finally destroying it in 146 B.C. The city burned for two weeks. Not one stone was left upon another, and the plain was salted to prevent the growth of anything.

Patton looks out at this eerie scene and declares, "I was here! Two thousand years ago I was here at the Battle of Carthage!" He draws intimately from the past, brings the past into the present, and uses that experience to prepare for the first American victory of the war at El Guettar.

You were there when Peter Waldo, John Huss, and William Tyndale began to rediscover the truth of Scripture, when the Pilgrim fathers were led forth by that Word, and when Jonathan Edwards proclaimed this truth. You were there with Lincoln as a lad and his family in the little Pigeon Creek Baptist Church in southern Indiana, at the Battle of Antietam, and when he gave the proclamation of 1862.

"Were you there when they crucified my Lord? Were you there when they laid Him in the tomb? Where you there when God raised Him from the dead? Sometimes it causes me to tremble, tremble, tremble!" You were there and shared in events of the past to the extent that your life has been influenced by them. Of all past events the most decisive are the death and Resurrection of Christ because His finished work can resolve the deepest dilemma of our lives, opening a way for us to have fellowship with God. Of all past events, only the acts of Christ can be rediscovered in their full consequences because He is a continuing Presence among us. The forgiveness and new life He offers are gifts for each of us to receive in the present with the open hands of faith.

There is a sense in which we cannot go back to any other event. The influence and consequence of an event cannot be completely rediscovered and appreciated. Only the finished work of Christ accomplished once and for all can be immediately rediscovered and appreciated in its full consequence for our lives. We cannot fully realize personally the influence of what happened at Appomattox in 1865 or at Milvian Bridge in 312, but we can discover the full significance of Calvary for our personal lives.

We can't go home to Greece or anywhere else. We go back to our boyhood home and we walk through the house in which we were raised. Suddenly it's as if we can hear Mother's voice, the sound of her step, and the presence of a simple peace we once knew. But we look about—the people are gone, the clock and the stove, the hedge and the lane are gone. It's not home. Can a man ever really go home? Home is people, home is roots, attachments, affection, where we like to be. Often these people and these places are suddenly gone. But there are new places and new people and someone calls, "Come home!" and we say, "I'll be there!" And we go home and it is precious. But eventually those closest are taken. We are left alone and it's not really home—everyone is gone. We all want to go home and be at home. There is a driving force within us when we are sick, lost, or lonely to go home. At such times we want more than anything else to come home. We have watched with tears of joy as prisoners of war have come home. The experience of coming home is precious to every one of us. And eventually the experience comes of not really being at home anymore.

It was to such people that Peter was writing, "exiles of the Dispersion," people who now found it difficult to be at home in this world. He was writing to both Jews and Gentiles in portions of Asia Minor where Christianity had spread very early. Most of the districts mentioned were represented among the pilgrims who were present at Pentecost and heard Peter preach on that eventful day. They were probably the first to bring the news of Christ to their homes. Jewish settlements abounded in those areas and through the synagogues Christianity first made headway. The problem of accepting Gentiles into Christian status was soon resolved and together their faith was built by teachers and prophets (*see* 1 Peter 1:12). We do not know if Peter visited those communities in the northern half of Asia Minor.

Edward Gordon Selwyn, in his commentary *The First Epistle of St. Peter,* argues that Peter's calling to "the circumcision" (Galatians 2:9), their need for apostolic guidance, and this first epistle make it quite possible that Peter visited the Christians to whom he was writing.

"Peter, an apostle of Jesus Christ, To the exiles of the Dispersion in Pontus, Galatia, Cappadocia, Asia and Bithynia." Peter wrote to people whose lives were in jeopardy because of their faith. Ever since this new faith had come to them they had not really been at home in their old surroundings. Things were radically different—they were "exiles of the Dispersion."

From the time of their captivity in Egypt, the Jewish people had longed for a home, a land, a name, an identity, and a future. That home was found in the Promised Land but the Jews never were completely at home in Palestine. They were dispersed by David and Solomon to Asia and Africa as government colonists and private tradesmen (see 2 Samuel 8; 1 Kings 4; 20:34). The Assyrian and Babylonian exiles were the chief cause of dispersion. The Assyrians destroyed the northern kingdom of Israel in 722-21 B.C. and carried a portion of its population into captivity. Judah, the southern kingdom, fell victim to the Babylonians, who forced most of the inhabitants of Judah to migrate from their native homes to Babylonia.

Now Peter writes to Christians, Jews, and Gentiles who are "exiles of the Dispersion," for they will never be completely at home on this earth again. They are being intensely persecuted. Peter speaks of their manifold trials (see 1 Peter 1:6). They are victims of evildoers and those who falsely accuse them (see 3:16). They are in the midst of a fiery ordeal (see 4:12). Their suffering can be endured only with God's strength (see 4:19). They will suffer for righteousness' sake (see 3:14). They are facing a campaign of slander and suffering. They can no longer feel at home in these surroundings. Peter says they are now pilgrims and strangers.

What does it mean to be a Christian? Peter says it means we have joined those people who are pilgrims. We have accepted an invitation to pilgrimage. We are exiles, aliens, and sojourners, strangers and pilgrims (see 1 Peter 2:11). The word is *paroikōs* in Greek—literally an exile away from home, a pilgrim in a strange land.

There is an important sense in which every Christian knows the warmth and the joy of home and at the same time he has the sense of being far from home. A young, attractive, skilled, capable couple just moved to our city. He has a challenging new job, they have a new house and a wonderful baby daughter. A year ago they accepted the invitation to enter the Christian life. He says, "My wife and I have never known what it is to be so close to one another. Our Christian faith has brought an inner depth to our lives and our relationship which is the greatest joy. Without the love and the faith God has awakened within us, life was a superficial, vain, senseless struggle. We know it is going to be difficult to do, but we have determined to put God first. We know that everything hinges on our faithfulness to Him."

These people have discovered the unsurpassed joy of the life into which God calls us, but they are living in the midst of a society and an environment in which the major influences work to obscure and replace the commitment and faith which have become the enriching, fulfilling center of their lives. In this world, at this moment, they have discovered the joy, worth, and fullness of life as God has intended it. But at the same time they are aliens and strangers in this world because this faith they cherish is foreign to their neighbors and business associates, as it is to the vast majority of people living upon this earth at this hour.

Men are still controlled by selfishness, greed, jealousy, hostility, materialism, and subtle injustices. These deteriorating forces will work to get a hold on this wonderful young Christian family and fill them with the dread, apprehension, uneasiness, and dissatisfaction plaguing so many who have so much in the midst of a foreign and hostile environment. They are pilgrims in this world. They won't flee from the world. They are going to enter into it deeply with their lives each day to work with all their skill and ability to realize the goodness of this world as God has created it. The Christian remains a stranger and an exile, a pilgrim and an alien upon the land which has been corrupted, polluted, and degenerated from the good in which God created it and to which it will one day be restored.

How will this young couple ever make it? Three months before they moved here a Christian friend who invited them into the Christian life told us of their coming when I was in a distant city. When they arrived, Christians, active businessmen in this community, received them, welcomed them into fellowship, encouraged them, brought them to church. They have entered into the fellowship of Bible study and prayer. They will be sustained and encouraged in their new walk with Christ, just as it was in the first century when the Christian faith challenged the world. As this is being written not only have they found life-sustaining fellowship but now they lead a small group for Bible study in their neighborhood and are providing encouragement to others.

We are troubled by the strife, discord, and distrust in our land at this hour. I hope this intense distress will serve to do one thing and that is to convince men that moral integrity, social justice, and sound government have a spiritual basis without which these values we cherish are impossible to maintain. Life's deepest convictions have a spiritual basis which demands the commitment, devotion, and eternal vigilance of all the people.

We are all the children of pilgrim fathers and for this each of us is grateful and proud. Whatever could have caused us to suppose this pilgrimage amidst cruel and hostile forces has ended. Once we cease to be moving forward spiritually we will fall backward morally. The prophet proclaimed to his people, "Woe to those who are at ease in Zion" (Amos 6:1).

The psalmist exclaimed, "Thy statutes have been my songs in the house of my pilgrimage" (119:54). "I am a sojourner on earth; hide not thy commandments from me!" (119:19). The writer of Hebrews knew that the patriarchs of Israel confessed that they were ". . . strangers and exiles on the earth . . . wherefore God is not ashamed to be called their God, for he has prepared for them a city" (Hebrews 11:13,16). The Christian knows his home is finally with God and that one day he will come home. The conflicts and trials of daily life do not leave him fragmented because he understands what is wrong with the world. He remains a whole person in a broken world, for he knows God has prepared a home for him. He knows that he has the privilege to be a part of the family of God because of what Christ has done to free him from the guilt of rebellion against God.

As Christians we discover the fullness of God's joy and promise in the depths of our experiences as the reality of Christ's love and presence come home to us. But as we live and work in this world we sense that we are far from home. We are pilgrims. We have a journey and a struggle with forces and enemies that are alien and foreign to everything godly, true, and just. We are thankful for the pilgrimage to which we are invited, for the love and joy we share now on this journey, and the assurance that at the journey's end we will be at home forever.

14

The Secret of a Balanced Life in a Troubled World

Blessed be the God and Father of our Lord Jesus Christ! . . . In this you rejoice, though . . . you . . . suffer various trials, so that the genuineness of your faith, more precious than gold . . . may redound to praise and glory and honor at the revelation of Jesus Christ.

1 Peter 1:3,6,7

Peter is speaking to people who are being confronted with the harshest possible affliction. It is sometime between the death of James in A.D. 62 and Nero's persecution in the summer of A.D. 64 The Christians are suffering various trials (*pĕirasmŏs, see* 1 Peter 1:6). This is the same word Jesus used at the Last Supper which refers to spiritual and mental trials as well as threats to His person (*see* Luke 22:28,40,46). This is the same word used by James (*see* James 1:2,12) for trial, testing, temptation directed toward an end. The purpose is that he who is tested should emerge stronger and more complete from the trial. These difficulties and sorrows are caused by opposition and are the means by which God tests (*dŏkimiŏn, see* 1:7) their faith which can emerge stronger, clearer, and firmer than ever. An athlete undergoes the rigors of training not to break himself but to develop more and more strength and staying power. Though hardships can be life-shattering and throw our lives completely off balance, Peter shows how these trials can be used by God to put strength into our lives.

The afflictions facing those to whom Peter writes arose from the sudden outbursts of persecution arbitrarily imposed by the whim of local authorities. Christians had to fear the fickle climate of public sentiment which ranged from casual indifference to blind hostility. Edward Gordon Selwyn, in his commentary *The First Epistle of St. Peter,* points out that when the emperor persecuted the Christians as Nero did in A.D. 64 and as Caligula had done twenty years before, the attacks by local authorities became more vigorous, frequent, and severe.

1. *Praise God and rejoice.* In the face of such danger and oppression how can the Christian's life and faith be refined, balanced, and strengthened? In the face of intense danger and suffering Peter opens his life in a doxology of praise to God: "Blessed be the God and Father of our Lord Jesus Christ!" (1 Peter 1:3). The secret of living a balanced life amidst the troubles of each day is to praise God for the new life and living hope He offers to us in Christ, who will never let this eternal inheritance be taken from us. Peter rejoices for the way in which God can use the harshest experience to strengthen and perfect our faith (*see* 1:7). Our faith is refined and purified under this testing and will finally praise and honor Christ for all He accomplishes in this present troubled world and in the new age which dawned with His coming and which will be fulfilled with His final return (*see* 1:8,9).

Every week I am with those who face sudden tragedy and the gravest disappointment. We can never be certain what will befall us within the hour, how radically different our situation may become, and what intense trial we may have to face. However, these persons who are trying to cope with a clearly defined hardship are by no means the most endangered among us. Indeed, they are frequently quite strong and joyful of spirit in spite of intense adversity.

There are countless others of us who have everything, who appear to be quite self-sufficient and happy, but who are walking on the fine edge of mental and emotional collapse. There is a constant, costly stream of petty pressures, tensions, irritating inconveniences, harmful hostilities, and devious thoughts. These tensions can take a momentous toll, leaving us more and more depleted, broken from within, unequal to what is demanded of us, unaware of the fabulous power by which new life and hope may be ours every morning. Through trials we can discover a source of strength and an ultimate purpose to the whole course of events.

How can rejoicing and praise rather than quiet desperation be the characteristic force in our lives? Paul says in 1 Thessalonians 5:18, "Give thanks in all circumstances. . . ." "Always and for everything giving thanks in the name of our Lord Jesus Christ to God the Father" (Ephesians 5:20). Now this is difficult to do and I am no master of the principle, but I am learning its power through the balanced lives of Christians who live vitally while under tremendous strain. When, in the midst of affliction, we can remain open in spirit rather than bitter, the renewing, sustaining, fulfilling power of God will control us.

Christ has one intention and that is not to make us miserable, but to make us more than conquerors in life. He has made inward peace and outward victory the inalienable birthright of every Christian. We don't have to stumble along from doubt, despair, defeat, and difficulty in bondage to circumstances. Rather we can see all these things brought under God's control and our joy may be full. Peter says, "Cast all your anxieties on him [God] for he cares about you" (1 Peter 5:7). Does anxiety plague you? Praise God! You have the opportunity to transfer your trust from every false security to the One who alone is worthy of your faith. Lord, teach me the secret of such vital living!

2. *Cast your cares on Him.* What is the first anxiety we give up, throw off, cast away with confidence upon God? Is it not ourselves, our own affairs and problems? Cast yourself, your fears, failures, faults, and feelings upon Him and leave them there. The Christian is one whose life has come under new management. Cast yourself in confidence upon the Lord. This is the beginning of victorious life in Christ.

Then give to the Lord every anxiety and leave each of them with Him. Many of us take our cares to God in prayer, but we are unable to leave them with Him—to surrender them to Him. We insist on taking these problems back to solve them in our own way and we are blind to the solution God has already initiated as a road to victory. When we cannot trust that God is working, we work our own defeat.

When we can put the issues of our life under His management we find the flow of strength that makes our efforts effective and our search a finding. He becomes the center of balance even when everything is going to pieces around us.

3. *Center down.* Our daughter Lynn loves horses. Why couldn't she like sewing or flowers? We learned that near where we vacation in the summer there is an outstanding riding instructor. So, Lynn and I have taken lessons. First, you have to get on the horse. This involves a certain amount of trust. When the horse begins to trot or canter you do not stay on by hanging on with pure physical strength. You center yourself over the horse in a balanced position so as to be coordinated with his movement. Then as you approach the cavalletti at the decisive moment before the jump, you don't hold back, which would be disastrous, but rather you give the horse full rein, lean forward, and let the force of his leap carry you across with him.

So we seek to become centered, balanced in God, coordinated with the force of His Spirit, confident that we will be sustained with clarity of thought and action even when most severely tested. Once we have practiced such trust our confidence grows with each trial and the genuineness of our faith is proved. The psalmist said, "Cast your burden on the Lord, and he will sustain you" (Psalms 55:22). Quakers like Thomas R. Kelly have helped us discover this principle of centering down in the holy silence, in the silent places of the heart, with complete openness ready to do, ready to live according to His leading.

Recently I talked with a man who is God-controlled—joy and confidence fill his life. He told me, "I can give thanks to God even as I face cancer for I know that my life and my future are in His care and I need not be controlled by the fear of this disease. I have learned what perfect peace and strength He gives." ". . . live for the rest of the time in the flesh no longer by human passions but by the will of God" (1 Peter 4:2).

Trouble comes, my job is threatened, a relationship brings continuous disappointment. These are occasions to rejoice and praise God for through them we may discover new depths of God's power as we become more deeply centered in Him. This discovery is through trust and the trial is the occasion through which that trust is made strong. "Let those who suffer . . . entrust their souls to a faithful Creator" (1 Peter 4:19).

When we go to the doctor, we must tell him everything, withold nothing, and we must follow his prescription specifically. We must put ourselves completely under his care. He is able to help us only when there is such total reliance. It is total abandonment unto the Lord which brings His joy within us and allows our joy to become full. Rejoicing before the Lord, casting our cares upon Him, and remaining centered in Him are the secret to a balanced life: "Come to Christ, who is the living Foundation of Rock upon which God builds . . ." (1 Peter 2:4 LB).

As we become centered in Christ, unhurried, peaceful strength increasingly fills our lives. Such life becomes amazingly simple, serene, and forceful because that life is oriented in one stream of influence which is as constant and infinite as God. Every occasion of life is set within a flow of power which makes the most of each moment and opens our lives to One who is timeless. There is no need to become frantic for we know who is in charge. We know that this day and every day opens unto eternity. We have the privilege to discover life's beauty and worth and to allow the serenity of Christ to become evident in our manner of living each day.

15

Shepherding

He himself bore our sins in his body on the tree, that we might die
to sin and live to righteousness. . . . So I exhort . . . [you] Tend
the flock of God that is your charge. . . .

1 Peter 2:24; 5:1,2

Shepherding is a biblical concept and practice expressing the style
and the strength of Christian fellowship. Jeremiah records God's
promise: "I will bring them [my people] back to their fold. . . . I will
set shepherds over them who will care for them, and they shall fear
no more . . . neither shall any be missing" (Jeremiah 23:3,4).

Shepherding in its practical and powerful dimension is being rediscovered today by the Christian community. In First Peter there are
two references to shepherding. First, we will consider the reference
in chapter 2 which gives the basis and model for shepherding. Second,
we will discuss the reference in chapter 5 which defines the work of
a shepherd. From these two passages we receive guidance for building
balanced and vital life within a congregation.

1. *The basis of shepherding.* "He [Christ] himself bore our sins in
his body on the tree, that we might die to sin and live to righteousness.
By his wounds you have been healed. For you were straying like
sheep, but have now returned to the Shepherd and Guardian of your
souls" (1 Peter 2:24,25).

The message in this powerful passage concerns Christ and what He
has done for us. He has taken the burden and the consequence of our
sin upon Himself. Everywhere people know something is wrong inside
themselves. Scandal, skepticism, and sorrow pour forth from within
us. The Bible teaches that this distorted condition of life is the conse-

quence of our rebellion against God. We are then bound to the guilt and power of sin, to a bad conscience and a troubled mind. And it is Christ alone who can free us. This is classically expressed in the great hymn "Rock of Ages": "Be of sin the double cure, Cleanse me from its guilt and power."

Cecil Osborne, in his book *The Art of Understanding Yourself,* says guilt is the primary cause of emotional and mental strain. The neurotic is one who has not been able to deal with his conscience, which is his own worst enemy. Christ cleanses us from our guilt when we rely on His forgiveness. This is a real cleansing, a real release. There is a self-destructive power holding us. Antagonistic thoughts and attitudes obsess us which are self-destructive and block the flow of God's Spirit into our hearts and minds. Christ frees us from this power when we rely on His strength. His intention is that we cast our burden, our sin, and our distress upon Him. This is the key step into the Christian life.

Quoting from the prophet Isaiah, Peter says, "By his wounds you have been healed" (1 Peter 2:24). Jesus intends that we cast our ills, hurts, troubles, anxieties, sicknesses, and burdens upon Him that He may help heal them, bear them, and overcome them. He is the Shepherd and Guardian of our souls. In Matthew 8:17 when Jesus was healing the sick it is recorded, "This was to fulfill what was spoken by the prophet Isaiah, 'He took our infirmities and bore our diseases.' " Jesus said of Himself, "I am the good shepherd; I know my own and my own know me . . . and I lay down my life for the sheep" (John 10:14,15). First of all, Jesus bears the burden of our lives. He is the basis and the model for shepherding. ". . . Christ also suffered for you, leaving you an example, that you should follow in his steps" (1 Peter 2:21).

2. *The work of a shepherd.* Second, we are called to bear one another's burdens. The second passage in First Peter about shepherding is 5:1-5: "So I exhort . . . [you] tend [shepherd] the flock of God . . ." not because you feel you have to or will get something out of it but because you are really concerned for their well-being.

The New Testament establishes the fact that Christ seeks to bear our burdens. Therefore, as Paul says, we are to "Bear one another's burdens and so fulfill the law of Christ" (Galatians 6:2). James says, "If you really fulfill the royal law, according to the scripture, 'You shall love your neighbor as yourself' . . ." (James 2:8). Jesus said to Peter, "Do you love me?" Peter said, "Sure, Lord, I love you." Jesus answered, "Feed my lambs, shepherd my sheep, tend my flock" (*see* John 21:15-17).

The Christian faith centers in the confidence that when we turn our troubles over to Christ, when we help one another, lives are built up, afflictions are lifted, burdens lightened, and lives are made whole. The pagan in the first century exclaimed, "Ye gods, how these Christians love one another." This comment was made concerning the very people to whom Peter was writing. Under the most severe affliction, an admirable quality of life was evident among them even to their enemies. Knowing that God cared for them, these early Christians were able to so care for one another that the imagination of the world about them was awakened. Jesus said, "By this all men will know that you are my disciples, if you have love for one another" (John 13:35).

At a very early date Christians came to learn that just as prayer and biblical living are means of grace (means through which God's grace comes to our lives) so is burden bearing. As we come to love and care for one another, the grace, the love, and the power of God are released into our experience, because we are obeying His commandment and claiming His promise. So when we genuinely care for one another in the Church, a far greater force than our own effort is released into our experience and applied to our problems.

When we cast all our anxieties upon God and are open to one another the power of God works mightily, effectively, and fully among us and this quality of life that builds up in our lives and relationships becomes the most powerful testimony and challenge to those within the world who wonder if the Christian faith has anything to offer to their lives. This quality of life within the fellowship is self-verifying.

A man would travel all the way across Chicago to attend the church where Dwight L. Moody preached. He was asked why he did this.

We would expect to hear,"Because I hear the Gospel there." This is the reason many people gave when asked that question. But this man's reason was, "I go there because they really know how to love a person."

The Christian is one who is vitally aware of an urgent and gracious Presence as the most important fact of his existence. To be aware of the urgent Presence is to know the imperative that is upon us and to be aware of the gracious Presence is to know the cleansing, restoring power sustaining our lives:

> "The Lord is my shepherd, I shall not want; He leads me in paths of righteousness for his name's sake. Even though I walk through the valley of the shadow of death, I fear no evil; for thou art with me. . . .

Psalms 23:1,3,4

Because the Lord is our Shepherd we are shepherds one to another.

Repeatedly in the history of the Church people have failed to remain diligent to the means of grace: prayer, biblical living, and burden bearing. A special office or class of individuals have then been designated to exercise these "religious" functions and they are called priests, pastors, and ministers. So when you need prayer you call upon a priest. When you want to understand something in the Bible, you call on a preacher, and when someone is in difficulty, you call for the pastor. As soon as these practices are neglected by the people and assigned to a group of specialists the Church, its members and those who accept this function are all left weakened and less vital.

You remember the figure of Walter Mitty, the great dreamer who would imagine himself performing some heroic feat. He pictured himself as a World War I flying ace. The crowds gathered just to watch him walk out as he put on his helmet, goggles, and scarf, and then they thrilled to the sight of his dramatic takeoff. Many professional ministers want to perform in this way. However, the proper imagery of the Christian ministry is not of a solo performance but of a whole squadron of airplanes soaring into flight, and this is precisely what is happening at this hour. We have rediscovered the ministry of the laity, the ministry of every Christian.

Laymen are coming alive in their personal faith. They are becoming proficient in prayer, biblical living, and mutual concern. Tremendous power is breaking forth into personal experience. The Christian life is not a matter of solo performance but of a shared ministry. The Greek word *diakonia,* which reads "ministry" in some English translations, literally means service. Every Christian is called into service and is a minister. So in Ephesians 4:11-13 Paul says that God grants particular gifts to some of us who are pastors, evangelists, and teachers, not so we can do the work of the ministry, but so we can help equip every believer to do the work of ministry, to build up the body of Christ until we all attain the measure of the stature of the fullness of Christ.

In the Presbyterian church I am a teaching elder. I am ordained to this office as some are ordained to be ruling elders and serve on the session. My role is to help equip you for your ministry, for the service to which God has called you and already endowed you with ability.

Convenant Church is seeking to learn how to meet the needs of people according to God's Word. Once this begins to happen we discover how intense the needs of every one of us are and people come from everywhere, for the needs of people are urgent and unresolved today. We find ourselves besieged with urgent requests which are beyond our strength to meet. The demand is beyond comprehension. The new life, strength, and courage people are finding is the most exciting thing anyone could witness. But so many of us are still seeking. First, we learn the urgency of human need, then we learn how vast and unlimited is God's love for us.

Just over a year ago we presented the challenge of shepherding according to the New Testament pattern to our congregation. I was reluctant to suppose that even twenty could be expected to assume this task. The hand of God has been on this venture as nothing I have ever seen. More than one hundred people are now serving as shepherds in this congregation. More than one hundred people have agreed to simply show interest, offer encouragement, and provide help whenever it is needed. They are not to carry programs, requests, or hidden agendas to their flock. They are simply there to help see that the needs of the Christian life are met. Each shepherd gives oversight to approximately ten families in a neighborhood. When difficulty comes the shepherd goes immediately and coordinates the service of the congregation to the person who is facing trouble.

One of the couples who are shepherds have experienced serious illness. He was in the hospital and uncertain of what would happen. One evening when he was unable to talk, another person came to visit him and simply said, "I'm a shepherd." He was comforted and encouraged. While he was in the hospital his wife continued to serve as a shepherd and is one of the most effective I have ever seen. People can really express their needs to her. She calls personally on every member of her flock. Recently when the shepherds met she shared what strength had come to herself and her husband through the small groups in Covenant before this difficulty and what love and power they have discovered coming forth through the prayers and concern of the people to strengthen them now. It became necessary for her husband to go to the Cleveland Clinic for open-heart surgery. She was to be with him through that ordeal. The recommendation is that two people be present with the patient. Their daughter who lives in Denver wanted to be present but was financially unable to make the trip. Members of the congregation provided the air fare for the daughter to be present with her parents. The daughter's husband exclaimed, "I didn't know churches did things like that!" The Crocketts are faithful shepherds. They have started a small Bible-study-and-prayer group in their area and unchurched people are discovering the vitality of Christian fellowship. Christ bears our burdens. Let us bear one another's burdens.

16

Building Balanced Relationships

Above all hold unfailing your love for one another, since love covers a mulitude of sins. Practice hospitality ungrudgingly to one another.

1 Peter 4:8,9

We have seen how suffering of the most intense sort was threatening the life of Peter and those to whom he wrote. Suffering impinges upon us. The shepherds in our congregation have been encouraging families facing a level of adversity few people suppose exists throughout an affluent community like ours. Personal trial and testing are a fact. Keith Miller, in his book *The Becomers,* says each of us is under a strain which continually threatens to become more than we can bear.

Writers invariably say suffering, pilgrimage, or hope is the central theme and concern of First Peter. In studying this letter I was surprised to discover that although suffering was the most immediate problem in Peter's life it was not Peter's central concern, nor was it the central theme of his letter. Peter's concern was with the full spectrum of the Christian life.

Building the immediate relationships of life is the subject given more attention than any other in Peter's letter. "Above all hold unfailing your love for one another." He is concerned about the relationships between Christians (*see* 1 Peter 1:22), between Christians and their enemies (*see* 4:16), between husbands and wives (*see* 3:1-7), between slaves and masters. And then even as they are suffering from the insane and senseless afflictions imposed upon them by Nero, Peter offers the startling exhortation, "Honor the emperor" (2:17).

Peter had discovered the key to personal victory over any circumstance. It's the same discovery being made by many people in our

111

congregation. The discovery we share with Peter is simply that, whatever the circumstances of our lives may be, personal health and strength are dependent upon building sound relationships with one another. Peter knew and we are learning that the most serious threat to our health and strength as a person is when resentment or fear, envy or hatred take over within. These negative thoughts and attitudes absorb our energy, leaving us bound to inner conflict, restricting the full flow of God's love and power within our lives.

Peter says, "Above all hold unfailing your love for one another." The Greek word translated "hold unfailing" (*ektenēs*) has a rich depth of meaning and indicates how sound relationships can be built in our lives. The word means to reach forth consistently and constantly. The imagery is of a horse at full gallop with consistent stride, of a runner reaching out at a steady pace toward a goal. The exhortation here then is to let our clear, consistent, decisive aim in every relationship become the responsible love offered to us in Jesus Christ. Reach forth with all that is in you to attain that mature love offered in the person of Christ.

1. *The journey inward.* When I make love my aim, part of me seems to say, "I'm not going! Count me out, it's not practical." We have the most intense difficulty keeping our whole being keyed upon this positive objective. Something always works to hold us back and flood our minds with conflicting thoughts. Therefore, students of the human personality through the centuries have recognized that the inner self is multiple, in conflict between a lower and higher, an inner and outer self. Paul exclaims, "For I do not the good I want, but the evil I do not want is what I do. . . . Wretched man that I am!" (Romans 7:19,24).

This summer in a distant place I was following a car. The driver was obviously confused and lost. He would speed up and slow down. My life was interrupted because of his distress. Finally he stopped right on the highway and then suddenly turned in the least likely direction. As I drove past, I put my head out the window and shouted, "Wah who!"

Good grief, what made me do that? Tremendous performance for a man of the cloth—great sensitivity, really holding fast to love. There is that within ourselves we don't like and we don't understand and here is our own worst enemy. Sin does easily beset us and remains the primary source of emotional and mental strain. One of the important advances in psychology has come with Hobart O. Mowrer, who has argued that the key to personal strength is not simply to dull the conscience, to remove or ventilate guilt feeling, but to acknowledge guilt to be real and to deal with it responsibly.

A key factor, then, for me in becoming a loving person is my relationship to myself. It is essential that I become honest and realistic with myself before God. I am in rebellion against God and at enmity with my neighbor. The principle model, then, for understanding myself is moral. There is a way of life in which we can stand. God is present and He is not silent. He has shown us the way in which to go. "Let the word of Christ dwell in you richly, as you teach and admonish one another in all wisdom . . ." (Colossians 3:16). But we rebel against this authority and devise our own ways. Our inner life is in conflict.

Peter says, "Love covers a multitude of sins." God reaches out (note the imagery again) and stretches across the chasm of my rebellion with His love to touch me. The question of my relationship to myself and to God is answered when I reach out to Him and trust what He has done in Christ to cleanse my life of the guilt and power of sin. My guilt is real, Christ's sacrificial death for me is real. His forgiveness becomes real to me when I reach out with the hands of faith to receive the love He offers. Christ Himself is the One in whom my whole life becomes centered.

In that moment, as I know God is reaching forth to me and that by faith I have reached out to receive, I no longer need to worry about the past or about my inadequacies because I know the direction toward which my life is pointed. I am becoming more and more authentic as a person. I will fall back and fail but I know where my goal is and I can come to respect myself because of the One for whom

I now live. The first step in building sound relationships is to become realistic about the conflict in myself and to recognize that the power of God's love can overcome that conflict.

When we journey inward through prayer, adoration, worship, and a gentle receptiveness to the divine Presence, our inner self becomes what Thomas R. Kelly, in *A Testament of Devotion,* calls a holy place, a divine center, a speaking voice which remains quiet and strong no matter what storms rage outside. The outward life is examined in the light of this inner Presence who enables us to see the whole of the world of men and things in a new way. The secular mind sees events and people in a limited perspective. The mind alert from within knows joy and peace, meaning and hope that the secular mind could never imagine. Resources of strength and confidence flow from within to an outward life of service and endeavor. A vital relationship remains between the inner and outer life.

2. *The journey outward.* The second step to building sound relationships is to reach out honestly, affirmatively, openly, vulnerably to others. We do not wait to take this step until we are completely at peace with ourselves and God. We do this at the same time that we are seeking to become more authentic as persons. Maybe it is difficult for you to accept the fact that I gave off a war whoop at a meandering motorist. But the important fact is that I cannot expect to relate to you on the basis of some phony perfection that simply is not there. Each of us has tension or conflict in our lives that we are attempting to resolve. If we try to form relationships acting as if that struggle does not exist we will never have an authentic relationship with each other.

When a young couple become attracted to each other on the basis of appearances and identify this desire as love, they have an affection which is without categories or content and when the weaknesses of their personalities become evident there is nothing to build on, the relationship is broken, and life is usually even more empty. The Christian centers his life upon love that is responsible and creative of relationship. Christ has put content into love so that love may become our aim.

114

The most decisive moment on the road toward personal growth and authentic self-identity before the world is when I drop my mask and reveal my deepest struggle to someone I can trust. We reach the point where we can be honest about our inner selves. But we do not dwell on the inner life—we move outward. We must go inward in the search for reality through prayer, worship, and study but the effectiveness comes when the inward is balanced with an outward thrust, when we go out in search of someone who needs encouragement. The glory of the Christian life lies in this combination of the inward and outward journey. Here is the key to a balanced life. It has to be!

We remember the childhood joy of possessing a secret we could choose to conceal or reveal. This is one of the most crucial privileges of the human personality. We have the need to conceal and to reveal. We approach self-identity and the point of building sound relationships when we make a free disposition of ourselves and find that confidence respected. In this experience of revelation and of being accepted we find the greatest encouragement for self-respect and respect of others. When through the love of God we dare to journey inward and then dare to journey outward in respect for self and for others we are building life in every dimension. "Above all hold unfailing your love for one another." Here are Christians who are under intense trial and testing. How natural for them to become tense and strained in their relationships. The problems could not be more overwhelming. Peter is telling about the great issues of faith and he says, "Practice hospitality." Why would he bring this in? When we look at it we see that this is the key because the relationships we share at home are the most precious. We learn at home the art of being a real person, of encouraging one another, and of making love our aim, which is life's richest privilege.

When the members of a family by the grace of God become honest with each other and determine to let the love of Christ dwell in them richly, they have developed a pattern of life which is the finest environment to enable someone else to see what Christianity is all about. It is a thrill to see a family share this quality of life with one another. Vivian and I found our relationship growing when we began to be free to share our deepest fears and needs, setting them before the authentic love in Christ. My son David and I enjoy a close relationship, partly because I tell him the things that worry me most and I encourage him to join with me in allowing our fears to become absorbed in the love of Christ. The inward and outward journey of a balanced life is learned best at home.

Recently two men visited with me in our home and we shared our plans, hopes, fears, and faith. We grew in our understanding of God's Word, of ourselves, our problems, and our possibilities. At the end of that time a high-school senior came to visit with me. My friends stayed to share with him, responding sensitively to the questions of his keen mind. The genuineness and depth of their faith were exhilarating to him.

Francis Schaeffer, who has practiced the principle of hospitality at *L'Abri* in a most dramatic way, says, "Do you want to change the world? Begin at home!" Let the love of Christ become the one all-encompassing force toward which you aim. Then invite others who are perhaps dirty or sick and let them share in the joy and richness of love which has become your goal and hope.

17

A Reasoned Faith

Always be prepared to make a defense to any one who calls you
to account for the hope that is in you, yet do it with gentleness and
reverence.

1 Peter 3:15

Do you hold a strong sense of hope within you? If you do, you are
unusual. People on every level of our society are despairing of ever
finding a sustaining sense of meaning for their lives. Those who possess hope will find it challenged. In sheer desperation someone will
cry out, "What's the use?" Or in bitter antagonism someone will scoff,
"How can you believe that stuff?" If I possess personal hope and am
not challenged, I have managed to spin a religious cocoon about
myself and to keep my faith under a bushel.

Many of us stand passive before the tidal wave of literature, film,
and news which proclaim a gospel of doubt, a religion of pleasure,
and a life of conflict. Who dares to enter the arena where public
opinion is shaped and begin to provide an alternative to futility? Sure,
there is an occasional Mary Poppins or Snow White. But remaining
in the eighth decade of the twentieth century who will provide literature possessing both the hope and the literary competence of Milton?
A teacher, a painter, an editor may stand before the seats of the
scoffers and offer a conviction for living. A mother will sooner or later
be asked, "Mommy, who made God?" or "Why can't Bobby walk?"
A businessman will eventually be confronted with the rationalization
"Go ahead, no one will ever find out about it." Each of us is called
upon to give a defense, a reason for the hope within us.

As you recall, Peter, who wrote those words, was writing to those who were being tested and tried for their faith. I have been arguing throughout our study of Peter that our faith is on trial and in severe jeopardy. The threatening forces are subtle and attractively disguised. Our attention is so absorbed by things, pleasures, and activities that the full content of our faith is gradually taken from us before we know it and we have not the strength of mind, will, or emotion to cope with life's demands. We sense that the vital balance is gone from us.

Peter says, "Always be prepared to make a defense . . . ." The word for defense in Greek is *apologia,* the word used by Plato for Socrates' famous defense of himself. It is the word used for Paul's defense of himself in Acts 22:1; 25:16; and Second Timothy 4:16.

From the word *apologia* we have an English word describing an important discipline of the Christian life. This Christian discipline is apologetics and has nothing to do with offering an apology for our behavior. Rather apologetics is the art and practice of defending the Christian faith, of rationally showing its validity in comparison to any alternative systems of thought or belief. The translation of this passage from First Peter in our Revised Standard Version fails to give the significance of the literal meaning of this passage which simply is, "Ready always with a defense for anyone who asks a reason for the hope within you." When we possess the basic hope of the Christian faith, how can we best give a reason for the hope within us?

1. First of all, we can best give a reason for the hope within us when we best *understand the role of reason* in bringing balance to the Christian life. Many of us are realizing that the Christian life begins when by the act of our will we put our trust in what Christ has done for us. Our emotions properly follow and are directed by that act of the will. But what about our minds? Do we leave them checked at the door when we enter the Christian life? No! With the act of commitment our minds are free to serve Christ. Reason is at its best when in Christ's service. The mind is free to pursue all areas of life. By reason a person can initially see the truth of God's Word; that what the Bible teaches is true to what is and valid for faith and life. Then by an act of the will a person may entrust himself to that Word of truth.

118

Reason goes in and out of vogue (like hair). For a time people trust in the power of reason to solve all the problems of life. But then they find that even people who claim to use reason will not act reasonably, and there is a retreat or escape from reason. Reason is out of vogue now and emotion is king. Rationalism is the tendency we all have of trusting reason to solve all of life's problems. Rationalism is the attempt, beginning with ourselves as our only reference point, to gain an understanding of all values and truth about life. So long as we remain egocentric our reason will bend, twist, curve, and turn things to ourselves. We can rationalize the most devious behavior and when it comes to Christ we will find every rational excuse and delay (we call them "head trips") for avoiding the surrender of ourselves to Him. When a man determines to become Christ-centered rather than ego-centered it's the most demanding decision of his life. It's as scary as getting married—trusting yourself to another.

Until I am Christ-centered my self-centered mind will make the acts of Christ seem foolish and the Word of Scripture nonsense. But when it is no longer I who live but Christ who lives in me the foolishness of the Gospel becomes the wisdom and power of God. In the service of Christ reason comes to the fullest light. Only in Him are we free to be truly reasonable and clearheaded. Reasonableness is a Christian virtue, and as we seek to give a reason for the hope that is within us, we seek the greatest clarity and consistency of thought possible concerning what we know and believe.

2. Second, we will best give a reason for the hope within us when we *understand the only assumptions upon which life can be lived* (upon which life can be based). The apologist is the most effective when he is able to see how unsatisfactory are the consequences of all alternatives to the Christian faith. Analysis on every level of our society reveals growing tension. Each of us is facing personal anxiety that we can scarcely bear. Why? First, I have trouble living with myself. Here is this self-will and it is self-destructive. But eventually I succeed at rationalizing some point of an egocentric adjustment. Then I try to justify this twisted view with others—TENSION—it won't work, it won't fit. Either my life, my family, or my affairs will go to pieces.

A young man claims there is no system of morals to which he is bound. Sooner or later he will appeal to someone for just treatment and he will have to face the fact that he has no claim to such consideration. The immoral life, the self-centered life encounters a tension it eventually cannot bear. A person has to come to terms with these consequences. We live in a theocentric, moral universe and only assumptions based upon these facts will hold up when applied to myself or others.

It is a traumatic experience when I view the real motives within myself. The Christian apologist is one who seeks to square his life with Christ—humbly grateful for what Christ has done. He then seeks to give a reason for the hope within his life and he is able to show that it is the only hope that makes sense. When we begin to help another person understand the consequences of the assumptions by which he lives it must be done with "gentleness and reverence," as Peter says. When a man finds the protective shield of his rationalization removed and his true motives revealed it is a terrible experience and more than many can bear.

So Christian apologetics is the art of gently but firmly helping someone else face the tension within his own presuppositions as applied to life. At all points I remain open to his questions. I refuse to withdraw from discussion demanding that he believe blindly or go by arbitrary authority. The demand to keep quiet and believe will lead later to spiritual weakness. I allow him to push me to the full consequences of the faith I claim and to ask me how well my life squares with these claims.

As I press the claims of Christ I must be ready to receive blows as well. But I keep pressing back, asking questions, for I know finally there is only One before whom all questions are answerable and as Paul said, "We destroy arguments and every proud obstacle to the knowledge of God, and take every thought captive to obey Christ" (2 Corinthians 10:5). We read in Acts how Paul went into the synagogue at Thessalonica and "argued with them from the scriptures, explaining and proving that it was necessary for the Christ to suffer and to rise from the dead . . ." (17:2,3). And when he argued with the "men of Athens" in the Areopagus, ". . . some mocked; but others said, 'We will hear you again about this.' But some men joined him and believed . . ." (17:32,34).

The Book of Acts concludes with the record of Paul in Rome ". . . trying to convince them about Jesus . . . And some were convinced by what he said, while others disbelieved" (Acts 28:23,24). Jesus asked the probing question of the apologist again and again as He sought to help men face the implications of how they lived: "And which of you by being anxious can add one cubit to his span of life?" (Matthew 6:27). "Why are you afraid, O men of little faith?" (Matthew 8:26). We best give a reason for the hope that is within us when first, we make reason the servant of Christ, and second, when we understand the assumptions by which life can be lived.

3. We best give a reason for the hope that is within us when *we help others find the joys of this Christian life.* A man may well decide that love is his thing although his love is without standards and seeks what it wants for itself. Sooner or later he will be faced with the consequences of any motive that sets its own standards and makes claims only for itself. It begins to break down. Perhaps one of you can be the one who helps him recognize the consequences in time. But selfish love, *eros,* is the blindest of motives and heaps upon itself the severest consequences.

At some moment each of us is ready to face the question, "What is love?" and at that moment we are ready for *agape* love which is concerned for the well-being of the other person, spontaneous, uncalculating, and creative of fellowship. We seek to apply that love. It's difficult to apply to myself, to others, and especially to an evil and ruthless world. But it fits, it works, it applies. When I am able to love someone else, when I am genuinely concerned for the well-being of another, a sound relationship is possible and for the frst time I can have a healthy respect for myself. And when this principle is applied to the world with all its unlovely ways, it's still the one possibility for hope.

"Ready always with a defense for anyone who asks a reason for the hope within you."

In 1952 when I was a philosophy major at Lake Forest College, I was elected a delegate to the Christian work camps in Europe. I was undeserving of the opportunity but it was God's way of opening my mind to the unparalleled validity of the Christian faith. I was assigned to a project in Belgium where we were to build a dormitory and dining room for a children's camp founded by Philippe Vernier.

During our briefing in New York, I began to hear the impressive stories concerning Vernier, who was a brilliant philosopher, a dedicated Christian, and a man of deep compassion who remained a source of strength to his people during the years of Nazi occupation. He is noted as a man of keen intellect and profound faith. He lives in a bleak coal-mining village where on the side of his home are the letters ABRI (shelter). People come in and out of this house for help at all hours.

I had just entered my tent at the Amougies camp in Belgium when a group of Boy Scouts burst in and their leader fell down beside me. To my amazement I learned that this was Vernier. I became acquainted with him as we worked together alone for five days digging the hole for a septic tank. He is the most unselfish person I have ever known. He is a clown, a saint, an author, a pacifist, a quiet, powerful, capable person. I watched him in keen debate with the Communists. I walked through the ruins of Europe, through displaced-persons camps, and gathered with small groups of Christians. The bleakest possible pessimism obsessed the minds of men everywhere, but among those who had lived and worked with Vernier there was unmistakable confidence and joy. They had been influenced by a man of reasoned faith. He possessed and had awakened in them a powerful faith in Christ. He was always ready to give a reason for the hope that was within him. Amidst the dark despair hanging over Europe I lived among a joyful and radiant people whose lives had been blessed by God magnificently through the humble life of one man.

In Philippe Vernier I found the single most forceful influence upon my personal life and vocational choice. I discovered the Christian answer to the desperate question of contemporary life. I discovered the balanced life of a Christian who is emotionally tender and sensitive to human need, who is intellectually tough when alternatives to Christ are discussed, and who gains inward strength through personal devotion. That inward strength finds decisive expression in a life of service as his devoted faith moves outward in dedicated love for others.

18

Equipped for Balanced Living

> After you have suffered a little while, the God of all grace, who has
> called you to his eternal glory in Christ, will himself restore, estab-
> lish, and strengthen you.
>
> 1 Peter 5:10

Suffering can strengthen us or it can break us. What faith we have
can be shattered or meager faith may grow from weakness to strength.
Peter faces formidable danger and he writes to those who confront
intense pressure. He is writing to us offering a word and a power to
undergird our lives.

In this verse there are three vivid and powerful verbs. Each of these
words portrays a vital dimension of the complete picture of what God
can accomplish in our lives even when we are confronted with the
severest suffering and trial. The words are Restore, Establish, and
Strengthen. You may become whole, well grounded, and empowered.
You will be equipped for living the balanced life (1) when you are
becoming a whole person, (2) when your life is well grounded, and
(3) when you are empowered.

1. First, life may become *whole.* The verb is translated in the Revised Standard Version as "restore" *(kartargein).* It is the word com-
monly used for setting a fracture. It is the word used in Mark 1:19
for mending nets. It means to supply what is missing, to mend that
which is defective, to restore the part that is lacking.

We are living in a time when lives become broken, fragmented, and
empty. We have been under duress from many sources and the least
provocation can cause us to go to pieces. We don't enjoy living on
the narrow edge of emotional exhaustion but that's where we are. We

live in the midst of broken lives, broken families, and broken relationships. Movies are designed to leave us shocked for the last time and stunned beyond the point of escape. We are stunned and we are shocked mainly with what we know about ourselves. When cover-ups fill the headlines we wonder how effectively our own ugliness is hidden. We live in the constant dread that people will find out what we are like behind our mask of self-sufficiency.

Advertising confronts us constantly with a picture of a beautiful person enjoying an attractively wrapped product. We try the product with all the outward poise and class we envy but we are still torn to pieces inside. We doubt ourselves and our adjustment to life. We strive even harder to appear neat, cool, and adequate in all circumstances regardless of how lonely or hopeless we are.

When we went on vacation last summer a couple came breezing over to introduce themselves and invite us for happy hour from five to seven each afternoon. Their gesture was absolutely genuine—they wanted friends and they wanted to be happy. The shock came of course when in the midst of happy hour the question was asked, "And what is your business?" Everyone listened, waiting for me to reveal a portion of myself. No one was ready for the revelation. When it came, it was too much. There was embarrassed silence as everyone tried to think of something religious to say. Someone managed to grunt, "Well, you don't look like a minister." That's a compliment.

The greater shock came when they learned that I could get just as aggravated with my kids as anyone else. Then we were able to begin to share about this new style of Christianity which refuses to be plastic, superficial, or false, which is open, honest, and responsive, seeking the wholeness which is personally present in the One who loves us and has given Himself for us, who seeks to restore wholeness to the depths of our lives, and who calls us to be utterly honest and candid before Him and one another. It's exciting then to see life become a great adventure rather than just a toleration of the whole mess until happy hour each day. People are seeking something that will speak deeply to their lives, giving direction and hope concerning their secret inner problems which they fear others will discover and reject them for having. There is no peace, no matter how impressive our facade. We remain uneasy that someone may really get to know us. We must break out of this plastic existence and be restored to the wholeness for which we have been created. The God of all grace will Himself restore you.

2. Second, life may be grounded upon a sure foundation. The Greek word is *sterizein* and means "to establish." James said to establish your hearts on the ultimate certainty (*see* James 5:8). Paul wrote, "For no other foundation can any one lay than that which is laid, which is Jesus Christ" (1 Corinthians 3:11). Christ is the One in relation to whom the pieces of life begin to fit together and make sense. The restoration of life within us comes when we began to establish and center down in Christ. The immediate opportunity for becoming thus established is to let the Word of Christ recorded in Scripture dwell in you richly (*see* Colossians 3:16). Our minds have been saturated and programmed according to a course of living that is defective and incomplete. Desperation is the outcome of the influences which besiege us. The Word of God is rich, demanding, and gracious and may become the reference point for our living.

We talked recently with a young woman who is a wonderful person of tender heart and a gracious life. She is married to a man who suffered intensely from irresponsible parents. He abhors his past, but he is breaking the lives of those about him for he accepts nothing but the rationalizations of his own mind and the inclinations of his own desires. His wife has a baby whom she is trying to raise and now her husband has his mistress living with them. This mother is brokenhearted, as are her parents, but she is determined now to set a foundation for her child that will sustain him amidst the shambles of life. She knows there is only one foundation that will hold up under the demands and that is the way of life offered to us in Christ and His Word. When any other alternative is propounded we must recognize that its end is the despair and futility gripping the lives of so many within our society today.

The Christian faith fills our hearts with compassion for one another, for every person whatever his outlook, commitment, or action. But this is not a naive permissiveness that condones all opinions and

126

accepts all viewpoints and actions as if they will sustain life. Jesus maintained a strong sense of outrage for every practice, for every false attitude, for every selfish rationalization and hypocritical pretense which causes life to become fractured, broken, and distorted. "You brood of vipers! how can you speak good, when you are evil?" (Matthew 12:34). The Christian remains compassionate of heart and tough of mind concerning the only foundation upon which the life of a man, a family, or a nation can be established and built.

3. Life may be strengthened. The Greek word is *sthenoun,* which means "to fill with strength." When that central commitment of our lives is settled concerning Christ and His Word, when we share that Word with one another and encourage one another to seek the Word, then the sufferings and afflictions, the disappointments and fears we have to face will lead us deeper and deeper into experiences of God's power. We will find ourselves being restored and made whole as we are established within the Word of Christ and are led from weakness to strength.

A woman found her way to the sanctuary over a year ago. She came each Sunday from some distance. Her husband had died in the prime of life from a terrible illness. She went to work and raised her children. Through her work she has lifted the lives of many people. She was visiting a family which was especially grateful for what she had done. When they asked her how she was able to do so much for so many, she told them of her personal faith in Christ. The family sensed something very exciting that was lacking in their lives. She invited them to come with her on Sunday morning. This family is now enthusiastic about a dimension of the Christian faith they have discovered in her which has now come to fill their lives. They are being restored, established, and strengthened as a family.

We were moved in February 1973 by the picture of Major McDaniel being greeted for the first time in seven years by his wife Jean, son Randy, and daughter Crystal. A photograph was released by Hanoi in 1969 of him leading fellow prisoners in a Christian song service. He tells of the "Zoo," the heartbreak of the six-foot-by-six-foot cells, the torture, uncertainty, and intense hardship of those years.

He relied in those days upon what had been instilled in him as a lad. He had whole passages of Scripture committed to memory. The North Vietnamese had Bibles but would seldom allow the prisoners to have one. He was called the memory bank. The verses he could recall were written crudely upon bits of paper and shared throughout the prison. Many lost faith when their prayers were not answered. Major McDaniel relied upon the Word and would not let divisiveness or doubt obsess him. His life and those about him were restored, established, and strengthened by the Word and the power he kept ever before them.

About two years ago a woman in our congregation experienced the most devastating loss possible in her life. Her husband simply informed her that he was leaving her for another woman. She had to face the one thing which above all else she would have asked not to have to face. There were areas of emotional immaturity and weakness in her life. I wondered how she would manage. She began to attend a prayer-and-Bible-study group. That group became the channel of God's love to her. Today she is a radiant, mature, confident person. She shared her story before a large group recently describing how her problems had seemed to be insurmountable. She took one day at a time, trusting that God would work out His plan for her according to His promise in Psalms 138:8. She found her problems being resolved. As she accepted what she did not want, her life was made complete through trial. A cherished relationship had been broken, but her life had been made whole.

God's fullest intention is that each of us live a complete life, lacking nothing. It is the God who has revealed Himself to us in the face of Christ who seeks to make us whole. He works to restore the defective areas within our lives. It is His intention that our lives become rooted, grounded, established upon a solid foundation. He seeks to give us the strength for abundant living. It is His purpose for us that we know the joy and fulfillment of becoming a whole person in mind, will, and emotion.